Classic Pathfinder 1

You speak, they speak

You speak, they speak: focus on target language use
(CLASSIC PATHFINDER 1)
Barry Jones, Susan Halliwell and Bernardette Holmes

Challenging classes: focus on pupil behaviour
(CLASSIC PATHFINDER 2)
Jenifer Alison and Susan Halliwell

Inspiring performance: focus on drama and song
(CLASSIC PATHFINDER 3)
Judith Hamilton, Anne McLeod and Steven Fawkes

Classic
PATHFINDER

1

You speak, they speak: focus on target language use

BARRY JONES, SUSAN HALLIWELL
& BERNARDETTE HOLMES

CILT
Centre for Information
on Language Teaching and Research

The views expressed in this publication are the authors' and do not necessarily represent those of CILT.

Acknowledgements

We wish to acknowledge the valuable and considerable contribution which the late Susan Halliwell made during her lifetime to the use of the target language, to classroom management and to the debate about the effective teaching of grammar. The new series of *Classic Pathfinders* allows another generation of language teachers to hear her voice.

In some cases it has not been possible to trace copyright holders of material reproduced in this book. The publisher will be pleased to make the appropriate arrangement with any copyright holder whom it has not been possible to contact at the earliest opportunity.

This compilation first published 2002 by the Centre for Information on Language Teaching and Research (CILT), 20 Bedfordbury, London WC2N 4LB

This compilation copyright © CILT 2002

On target: teaching in the target language first published 1991; second edition 2002; © CILT 1991, 2002

Keeping on target first published 1994; second edition 2002; © CILT 1994, 2002

Illustrations by Caroline Mortlock (pp12, 16, 17 and 18) Dandi Palmer (pp20, 41 and 42)

ISBN 1 902031 99 7

A catalogue record for this book is available from the British Library

Printed in Great Britain by Cromwell Press Ltd

CILT Publications are available from: **Central Books,** 99 Wallis Rd, London E9 5LN. Tel: 0845 458 9910. Fax: 0845 458 9912. Book trade representation (UK and Ireland): **Broadcast Book Services,** Charter House, 27a London Road, Croydon CR0 2RE. Tel: 020 8681 8949. Fax: 020 8688 0615.

Contents

Foreword

The first in the new series of *Classic Pathfinders*, *You speak, they speak* addresses the issues of teaching through the target language and progression in pupil use of the target language. Is it really necessary, now that the National Curriculum is well established, to turn our attention to these issues once again? We believe so and we will tell you why.

The first reason is to take stock of where we are now. Much has been achieved since those early days, when it was less common to teach through the target language. Most teachers nowadays conduct their lessons in the target language and the majority of pupils accept this as normal. Even the boys can cope. Recent research into boys' performance [1] confirms that teaching through the target language is not in itself perceived to be a problem. And yet, if we think about our pupils overall and how much they use the target language for themselves, we would probably all agree that there is still some way to go.

What does OFSTED have to say about this?

- *Pupils need to develop the 'productive' skills of speaking and writing in the foreign language.*
- *Many pupils have an underdeveloped capacity to initiate and develop conversations.*
- *They find difficulty in developing strategies to deal with the unpredictable.*
- *They are not offered adequate opportunities to adapt language and apply it to new contexts.*
- *In some instances there are limited opportunities to ask and answer questions.*

Excerpts taken from Secondary Subject Reports 2000/1 OFSTED HMI 383

What kinds of interaction are we talking about? What can we do better?

It would seem that at present, to varying degrees, pupils are using unanalysed chunks of language in partner work and routine phrases to make simple requests in the classroom. But they could do more.

In our recent work with student and graduate teachers we have seen excellent examples of how in very simple ways pupil language is being extended through:

- encouraging structural complexity by the use of prompts such as *et, aussi, mais, puis;*
- using 'real' as opposed to scripted feelings in genuine social interaction with pupils;

- eliciting spontaneous reactions to the unpredictable set up by pupils in role-plays;
- making jokes in the target language by inventing new words in humorous reconstructions;
- exchanging points of view about topical events;
- making decisions and justifying choices;
- evaluating each other's performance or creative writing in peer assessment.

The key questions will always be:

- Where does the language come from to support pupil use of the target language?
- How do we start this process?

There are no simple solutions but we could consider:

- modelling pupil language from teacher language;
- explicit teaching of interaction or task-specific language;
- increased use of real world contacts to stimulate communication;
- learners learning from more capable learners in mixed-ability situations.

This book gives examples and discusses these matters further.

The second reason is that the impetus of the National Literacy and Key Stage 3 strategies, with their focus on meta-language and meta-cognition, may encourage us to increase the amount of time spent in lessons talking in English about language and about how we learn. This could represent a paradigm change in the communicative classroom. The time is ripe to re-open discussions about the philosophy of foreign language teaching and learning and how it differs from mother-tongue teaching. The question will be to decide when the use of English is really necessary and when such discussions can legitimately take place in the target language.

It might be necessary initially to use English in the following circumstances, when requiring learners to:

- identify and reflect on learning processes that are new concepts to them, e.g. discussing how they read a text and identifying reading strategies; exploring techniques for memorisation;
- spot patterns and make analogies to Language 1;
- handle socio-cultural issues, requiring learners to address their own values and those of others.

However, as learners progress, such issues can increasingly be tackled using the target language.

We feel that *You speak, they speak* tells a convincing story of how to develop an ethos of communication in the target language, involving teacher-to-pupil, pupil-to-teacher and pupil-to-pupil interaction.

Part 1: *On target* demonstrates how it is possible to teach through a language that the pupils do not yet know and suggests very practical strategies for teachers, for learners and for the department as a whole to begin the process of using the target language more consistently and more frequently to conduct the business of the classroom. The emphasis is very much on using the here and now, focusing on the learners' direct experience in the classroom as the main stimulus for language use.

Part 2: *Keeping on target* builds on this strong foundation and considers how to extend the range of experience that pupils have in using the target language to their teacher and to one another. It explores the nature of challenge, questioning and linguistic progression, taking a closer look at the kinds of activities that involve learners in stepping beyond the basic response. We can see how pupils can develop their ideas, using language creatively and discursively in individual, pair and small group work.

We have set out to provide access to theory, practical guidance for planning and examples of stimulating ideas for teaching and learning that have been tried and tested in classrooms. We believe that it is possible to support learners to learn about language and through language in a classroom where the target language is the natural means of communication. We hope that we can persuade you to agree with us.

Bernardette Holmes
Head of Professional Advice, CILT

1 Jones, B. and Jones, G. et al (2001), *Boys' performance in Modern Foreign Languages: listening to learners.* CILT.

Part 1

On target
Teaching in the target language

BARRY JONES
& SUSAN HALLIWELL

Introduction: making the language real

We have set out to do three things in Part 1 of this book:

- to show how it is realistic and possible to teach in the target language;
- to propose effective strategies;
- to offer some suggestions for departmental workshops on the theme.

The National Curriculum for England for Modern Foreign Languages requires that:

> *During Key Stages 3 and 4, pupils should be taught the knowledge, skills and understanding (as set out in the Programme of Study) through:*
>
> a *communicating in the target language in pairs and groups and with their teacher;*
> b *using everyday classroom events as an opportunity for spontaneous speech;*
> c *expressing and discussing personal feelings and opinions;*
> d *producing and responding to different types of spoken and written language [...];*
> e *using a range of resources, including ICT, for accessing and communicating information;*
> f *using the target language creatively and imaginatively [...];*
> h *using the target language for real purposes;*
> i *working in a variety of contexts [...]*

> *(DfEE 1999: 17 para 5)*

We believe that this requirement is best met if we teach our classes, as often and as systematically as we can, using the target language as our main and sometimes exclusive means of classroom communication. This is not to ban the use of English. To do so would be dogmatic. We would, however, only aim to use the learners' mother tongue to fulfil certain, well defined purposes. These may include discussion by pupils and teachers of grammatical features, concepts and understanding or of their developing learning and study strategies, or of their understanding of 'otherness'. Even these aims, as have been described elsewhere (see Harris, Burch, Jones and Darcy 2001), have been successfully met by using the target language.

WHY?

There are four main ways in which it will help our learners if we teach them in the language they are learning.

- They need to experience the target language as a **real** means of communication.

- If we teach them in the language they are learning, we give them a chance to develop their own in-built language learning system.

- By teaching through the target language we are bridging that otherwise wide gap between carefully controlled secure classroom practice and the unpredictability of real language encounters.

- By encouraging pupils to understand and use the target language – at times, a struggle – we are seeking to develop strategies for listening and strategies for expressing meaning when they may only have limited language available.

MAKING THE LANGUAGE REAL FOR THEM

It is not enough for us to keep pointing out to the learners that real people 'out there' actually use the target language both in daily speech and for normal understanding. Nor does it make much impact to say that at some later stage in their lives they themselves may really need to use it in both those ways. Both those concepts are too distant. We need to make the language real here and now. By teaching in the target language we can make it something that they themselves experience and use today. It is not just a vehicle for exercises and activities, to be put into real use sometime later.

HELPING THEM TO LEARN BY EXPERIENCING LANGUAGE AS WELL AS BY CONSCIOUS LEARNING

Until relatively recently, language classes have tended to operate almost exclusively as occasions for conscious learning and practice. The focus has been on deliberately working things out as accurately as possible. But we all know that there are other ways in which we can acquire a language. As part of our own language experience we have learnt a foreign language not only as a result of someone else's teaching but by finding ourselves in situations where it is being used around us. We get it by experimenting with it and living it as well as by studying it. Our learners bring this same dual capacity with them to the foreign languages classroom. By teaching in the language we are giving this powerful system a chance of operating alongside deliberate language learning.

As they try to make sense of and find patterns in the language they encounter and use, they acquire language. It is, after all, this ability to apply in-built learning strategies which helps learners learn more than they are taught. It is certainly the case that they learn, too, in ways other than those which we decide for them.

BRIDGING THE GAP

In real life, speakers of a foreign language often have to cope with not understanding everything they hear or read or with not being able to say exactly what they want. It will help our learners if right from the start we build up their confidence in this respect. They need to learn to take risks, both in understanding and in speaking. They need strategies for getting by. Teaching them in the target language prepares them for this.

1 What makes it possible to teach in the language they have not yet learned?

It is important to remember that messages are not carried by words alone.

Some teachers have one or more of the following reservations about teaching in the target language.

- They worry that children won't understand and won't know what to do.
- They worry that because classes resent being put in this position they will misbehave.
- They worry that they themselves sometimes do not know enough of the language to be able to do it effectively.

These worries arise because, as teachers whose work relies so heavily on words, we can easily forget two things. Firstly, nobody needs all the words they hear to understand perfectly what is said to them. Secondly, there are other sources of meaning. Even in our mother tongue a great deal of our understanding comes from our ability to interpret messages independently of the words. In fact, we often rely quite heavily on what we think the message is about rather than what is actually said. (This process is so common and so effective that most of the time we do not notice that we are doing it. In fact, it is most noticeable on the occasions when we get it wrong!)

We do not just take meaning **from** language; we also take meaning **to** language. There is a kind of reinforcing reciprocity.

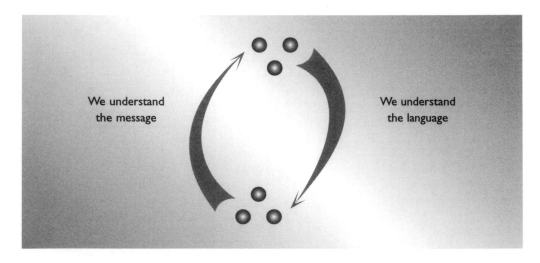

We understand the message

We understand the language

Among other things we take the message from:

- the immediate context;
- our knowledge of how the world works;
- demonstrations;
- our reading of intonation patterns/facial expressions/general body language, etc.

The immediate context

Imagine you are standing watching someone you know doing some woodwork. They hold out their hand mumbling something through a mouthful of nails. You are unlikely to think that they are offering to shake hands. Even if we do not hear a word, our understanding of the immediate context is likely to make us hand over a hammer.

Knowledge of the world

We learn from experience to expect people to behave in certain ways in certain situations. In terms of the classroom that means that the learners have expectations about teacher behaviour. So, for example, if a teacher walks across to one of the class and hands over a pile of worksheets, few children would think of asking what they have to do with them. They know. Indeed, these anticipated messages are sometimes so strong that the class ignores what you actually tell them to do and does what they expect you to want them to do. Even in the mother tongue the role of the language is often simply to confirm a message already received. In the case of a foreign language, the message we have already received will enable us to understand and to process the language that comes with it. For most schoolchildren this 'knowledge of the world' is still closely culturally determined. The more they encounter a foreign language in a cultural context the better they will interpret it when they meet it for real.

Watching for meaning

Words on their own are a poor source of information. Imagine being instructed over the phone how to change a nappy. We are much more likely to be able to follow instructions if we can see someone doing what we have to do.

Interpreting social signals

From our earliest days we read the messages from facial expression, gesture, body language and intonation. Irritation or encouragement, determination, enthusiasm and amusement do not need words.

Because the message is carried and interpreted through these and other channels, it means that in the classroom:

- the learners can understand what is going on even if they don't yet know the words/structures (that is why it is possible to teach complete beginners in the language they are learning);
- the teacher does not have to be a fluent bilingual, able to say anything and everything in the target language. Limited language can carry quite complex messages.

In fact, some people believe non-specialists are often at an initial advantage over the native speaker. Although this may not be so, they are **trying** to do two crucial things:

- to go for clear messages in limited language, whereas the native speaker or highly skilled specialist tends to talk on, relying on words because for them they **do** carry the meaning. This is worth remembering if we are in the fortunate position of having a Foreign Language Assistant in the school. Simplifying the language is something she or he will probably need particular help with;
- to provide a parallel source of information by means of actions, demonstrations, gestures, facial expressions, etc.

So we need to remember that we do not need to put into words everything in the target language which we would have said in English. In fact, if we do try to operate through the equivalent amount and the equivalent complexity in the target language, we can make life very difficult for the learners. They will then probably respond by making life difficult for us! Of course, as the classes understand more of the language and get more used to the situation, we can begin to rely on more words and to use more complex language, which we can build up systematically. Meanwhile, to begin with we are trying to get the message across in two main ways in order to do three basic things:

source	to convey
• messages without language • messages through limited language	• what is happening • what the class has to do • the fact that everything is under control

PROVIDING MESSAGES WITHOUT LANGUAGE

Two key features help here:

* breaking things down into short easy stages;
* 'telling' by showing and doing.

These are in fact simply extending something we all do already in our teaching. If we watch good teachers teaching any subject in the mother tongue, they rarely describe a whole activity in one go and then expect the class to remember the whole thing. They are much more likely to set the activity up in small, clearly defined stages. They also very often do what they are talking about as they speak. If we do this in a language class, it is not just a longwinded way of going about it. In the process of setting the activity up by doing it we are:

* confirming the language patterns both for understanding and for the use that is about to follow;
* establishing more clearly than is possible with words alone, what the class has to do.

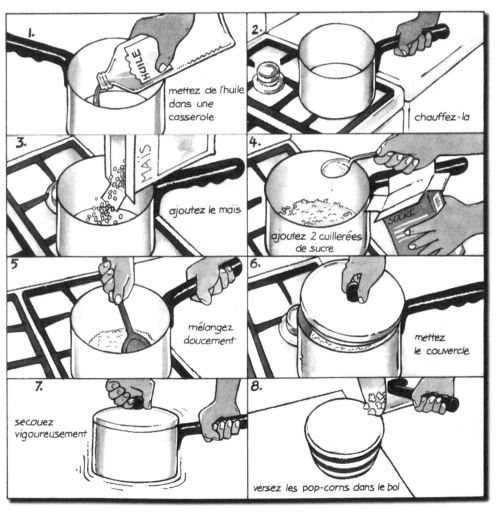

Spirale 2: Overhead transparencies (Jacqueline Jenkins and Barry Jones, Hodder & Stoughton, 1993)

In the example on the previous page we have temporarily omitted any language other than the language being practised. This should illustrate how the message about what to do and how they should do it is carried by what the learners **see**.

It is quite common for textbooks or real first aid leaflets to describe ailments and injuries and their treatment by a series of numbered pictures. In the initial stages of teaching these we want the learners to recognise the sound of the phrases and mentally match them up with the event depicted. We can set up an activity to do this, entirely on the explain-by-showing-and-doing principle. If you were using an authentic leaflet the activity could go like this:

- Hold up the leaflet and point to the appropriate page of the pictures (labelled a–j). Hold it so that the class can see whether they have found the right page on their photocopy.

- Write the numbers 1–10 on the board.

- Say aloud one of the phrases.

- Search **obviously** for the picture which matches the phrase.

- Write the letter of the matching picture alongside 1 on the board.

- Repeat the process for a second phrase. By the time you get to the third phrase the learners will be anticipating and will tell you which letter to write up.

- Pick up someone's exercise book and hold it up.

- Open it at the back.

- While the class gets organised rub out the preliminary examples.

- Point to the numbers 1–10 and indicate that they should write out a similar list.

- Start again with a new phrase. (For the first two watch to see that they have got the idea and to confirm, for the slower ones, that they are on the right track. We can do this by again writing up the answers. After that we can leave them to it.)

Written out like this it looks almost insultingly obvious. Yet it is precisely this kind of very simple system of non-verbal messages which enables us to teach even complete beginners in the language they are learning. Instead of trying to give all the information about the activity at the beginning, it has been built up stage by stage by actually **doing** it. At each stage the necessary information has been **seen**. This does not mean that the teacher is just relying on gesture and miming. The whiteboard or OHP also acts as a very important source of visual information and instruction by example. The strategy also mirrors what teachers of other subjects often do when giving complex instructions or information so does not appear odd or out of place.

The same very simple process underlies all teaching in the target language. It is even **more** important, not less, when setting up more complicated activities and it remains crucial even when increasingly complex language is added.

By working in this way we are not just enabling our learners to cope with the target language. We are actively helping them to acquire it. A TV cookery demonstration is understandable with the sound switched off. Accompany it with language and as well as the cookery techniques the associated language is learned. We should not be too concerned that we do not know if **all** our learners in this situation are acquiring the **same** language, or, indeed, if they are acquiring **all** of it. What we can guarantee, however, is that, without it being systematically taught and practised, all of them will learn something that they would not otherwise have learned. In other words, learning can take place **without** explicit teaching and often without a learner immediately realising what he or she has learnt.

We can now look at some strategies for adding limited language to the messages which are already carried by what the class can see and can predict.

PROVIDING MESSAGES WITH LIMITED LANGUAGE

It helps to:

- avoid long bursts of language without other sources of message;
- keep eye contact in silences and voice contact when looking away;
- use volume, intonation, emphasis and repetition to highlight meaning;
- use cognates – in written form – initially where they exist;
- use marker words to convey the structure and a sense of purpose;
- signal the general nature of each activity;
- use **single** words, initially, to signal the specific nature of what you are about to say;
- use a small selection of all-purpose phrases
- if English surfaces use it indirectly.

We will look at each of these separately and then see what they look like as a whole.

Keeping it short

A long flow of the foreign language without any other source of message, particularly at the beginning of the lesson before the learners are tuned in, can produce panic and resentment. It helps to keep the message pithy and to use something else to back it up.

Instead of ...	Try
Aujourd'hui on va écouter une conversation entre Astérix et Obélix. Ils sont dans leur village en Bretagne. Bien! Je vais jouer la cassette. Puis vous allez répondre à mes 10 questions. Bien! Sortez vos cahiers et écoutez la cassette. Ça va?	**1** *Regardez, voilà Astérix voilà Obélix.* (write names on OHP or board) **2** *Ils parlent.* (mime) **3** *Ils sont dans leur village.* (show) **4** *Voilà des questions sur la conversation.* (show on OHP) **5** *Ecoutez la cassette.* (show, mime) **6** *Ecrivez les réponses dans votre cahier.* (pick one up)

Keeping in contact

One of the problems of reducing the flow of language is that many of us have learned to express our classroom personalities through the style of our English. How does one convey the equivalent of 'Watch it!' in French ...? If language is limited, contact can seem limited for both parties. It is therefore all the more important that the teacher does not 'disappear'. If the class is feeling insecure it is more likely to switch off. We have got to signal somehow that we are still with them. After a while this will cease to be a problem. Once we and they are used to working in the target language, our classroom personalities emerge as clearly as ever. Meanwhile, however:

- when there has to be a silence, perhaps because we need to give them time to think ➤ it is even more important that we look at individuals round the class;

- when we need to turn our attention away from them ➤ it helps to use filler phrases to signal the pause is intended, e.g. *attendez une minute* ... and/or to comment in the target language on what we are doing as we do it, e.g.

(drawing grid on the board) *bon voilà une ligne verticale ... et puis encore une ... voilà la troisième ... et maintenant les horizontales ... une ... voilà ... deux ... et ... trois ... Ça y est!*

Providing stepping stones

It will help the learners if we make key words stand out in some way. We can make them louder, more emphatic, or we can combine either of these with a pause. In this way we provide stepping stones of meaning through a flood of language. Equally importantly, by doing this we are also building up the learners' willingness and ability to predict and to work on the basis of partial understanding.

Building on what they already know

Sometimes there is a word which **sounds** sufficiently similar to the English to help understanding, especially if accompanied by confirming mime or gesture, e.g. *copiez … on change …* Sometimes the cognate exists but would not be so readily used by a native speaker, e.g. *stop!* … In the latter case we can use the cognate initially and attach the less familiar word to it. Later, we can leave the new word to stand on its own, e.g. *Also, jetzt kopieren … nachschreiben … ja, nachschreiben … kopieren …* If the cognate is clearer when **written,** we can provide the written word on the whiteboard **at the same time** as we speak it. Although this tactic can undo developing sound listening strategies, it can be used when it is really helpful and/or the message has to be clearly understood, such as when setting homework, etc.

Providing a clearly structured framework to what is going on

Little words like *jetzt, also, aber, inzwischen* in German and *d'abord, finalement, deuxièmement, maintenant, mais* in French, have the same effect as paragraphs have in writing. They show beginnings, endings, changes of focus, relationships between sections. They can signal that what is about to come is important. They say to the class *'come back in even if you switched off earlier'* or *'make sure you don't miss this bit.'* They refocus attention. They also give a comforting sense of shape and purposeful progress to the lesson. They also provide models of language which learners will begin to use for themselves, especially if encouraged, as familiarity and confidence increase. It can be very motivating to reward such use of the foreign language **publicly**. This may be done with a system of *Bons Points*, wall charts recording pupil use of this kind of language, class monitors who record such events on behalf of the teacher, or other ideas which reflect a school's policy on rewarding achievement. (*Bons Points* have been used for many years by David Williams, Head of Modern Languages, at the Neale Wade Community College, March, to whom we are indebted for the idea.)

Signalling the general nature of the activity

Words like *écoutez, regardez, dessinez, travaillez avec un(e) partenaire, test ... aufpassen, hinsetzen, hinschreiben, Partnerarbeit,* etc provide something immediate and simple to respond to. They provide the first-line security of knowing roughly what is going on. The more the learners understand what is going on, the less likely they are to look for an excuse to misbehave.

Indicating the nature of the language utterance that is about to come

We often know what an utterance must be (e.g. question or answer) because we know what it means. But we have all seen classes sitting there wondering whether they have to repeat, answer or do something. So it will help them to know what sort of utterance is coming if we use cues like:

écoutez ... question: ...

maintenant ... exemple: ...

Using an initially small set of key phrases

It is worth remembering how few phrases we actually need. We are often very wordy in our mother tongue. Whereas in English we might say:

'Can you stop and listen, whether you have finished or not', in French this can become simply, *'Bon, écoutez'.*
Or
'Now I want you to do this in pairs' becomes *'Jetzt, Partnerarbeit'.*
Or
'Let's have a bit of hush for a while, you lot' shortens to *'Du calme!'*

Even more basically, *oui, non, mais, also bitte, na so was, faites comme ça, ne faites pas comme ça,* etc can be used for a whole variety of occasions including some of the less comfortable moments in a classroom.

Different intonation can also often extend the use of a single phrase. *'Was ist los?'* or *'Tu as un problème?'* can be genuine enquiries. They can also be a reproach or a reprimand. This use of intonation to extend the use of a limited range of language is something learners need to learn to do themselves in order to get by with limited language, so it is all to the good.

If this key language is, initially, kept both simple and consistent, it can be recorded by the teacher on an Overhead Projector Transparency (OHT) in the form of an ever-growing list. If learners have a problem with comprehension or recall, it can be referred to as the need arises. Such a list, if kept with lesson notes of each class taught, can help with revision, be used for spelling practice and, if appropriate, can show grammatical features already used with confidence **before** more formal grammatical teaching, analysis and explanation takes place in class.

Using English indirectly

There will inevitably be moments when English does arise naturally. Textbooks may have passages of English by way of background or explanation of grammatical points. Without going into contortions, it is possible to use these but still to restrict the amount of English used.

For example: *Regardez la page xx. Lisez l'anglais en silence.* (later) *Bon ... question numéro 1.* (child answers in English) *Oui, c'est ça ... Quand le substantif est féminin on met un e.*

There are also occasions when we will want to be absolutely sure that no one has the excuse later of claiming that they did not understand, for example in the setting of homework. Even this is not a problem in the target language once the class is used to the system. Meanwhile, as an interim measure we can use the board to provide a simultaneous parallel, e.g.

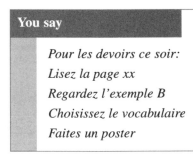
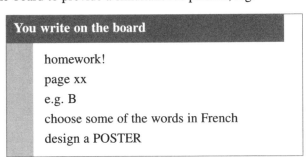

You say	You write on the board
Pour les devoirs ce soir:	homework!
Lisez la page xx	page xx
Regardez l'exemple B	e.g. B
Choisissez le vocabulaire	choose some of the words in French
Faites un poster	design a POSTER

Alternatively, one of the class can be used as a 'class interpreter' so that he or she has to summarise in English what has just been said. (This is interpreting for real, not just translating.) Finally, if single words in a text are proving a stumbling block, there is no point being fanatical. After all, no one is asking you to spend half an hour trying to demonstrate the word hippopotamus or *'ensuite'*! Similarly, if a learner does not know a word in the target language, why should we object to something that comes out like *'Je n'ai pas de felt tip'*? A reply *'Ah, tu n'as pas de stylo feutre'* combined with handing one over will supply both the missing word and the pen in a combination which is likely to be remembered.

However, we need to monitor this carefully. If we find ourselves supplying English words frequently, it is the beginning of the slippery slope to defeat. It does **not** help at any stage to:

- keep asking if they understand
  (They are not going to understand everything so they will play safe and say no. This is very defeating for both teacher and learner. In fact, they will nearly always have understood enough and we can see if they understand by the way they react.)

- check constantly for exact meaning and translations
  (Again this implies that they have not understood unless they can reproduce it exactly in the mother tongue. We know from our own experiences that there are occasions when we have understood but cannot find the exact mother-tongue words.)

- keep switching in and out of the target language
  (If we do this, we easily destroy both the urge and the opportunity to deal with the foreign language. Learners will simply operate with the English.)

Here are two examples of all these ideas put together. The first example suggests what could be done to set up a pairwork activity using the textbook. This assumes there has already been a lively introduction, using mime, objects and actions, to provide a clear explanation of the appropriate language below:

A	B
une coupure (pas trop grave)	lavez la blessure avec du coton passez une pommade antiseptique couvrez avec un pansement, ou un sparadrap
un bleu	trempez du coton dans de l'eau froide et propre mettez un pansement
un mal de tête	trouvez des cachets d'aspirine lisez l'étiquette donnez la dose correcte
une brûlure (pas trop grave)	mettez de l'eau très froide séchez avec soin couvrez avec un pansement sec
une piqûre d'insecte	mettez de l'eau froide passez une pommade antiseptique

Now we want to set up the pairwork.

4 Etes-vous secouriste?

Travaillez avec un partenaire.
Votre partenaire couvre la colonne A. Vous couvrez la colonne B.

Vous dites:
Pour une coupure?
A tour de rôle!

Votre partenaire dit:
lavez la blessure
passez une pommade
couvrez avec un pansement, etc

From *Jeux de mots* by Barry Jones,
Cambridge University Press, 1987

Colonne A	Colonne B
une coupure	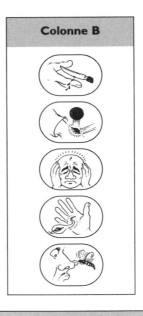
un bleu	
un mal de tête	
une brûlure	
une piqûre d'insecte	

	Words	Actions
1	*Maintenant ... regardez ...*	Hold up your book.
2	*A la page 16.*	Open your own book at 16 and turn it so they can all see the page.
3	*Exemple.*	(You could write e.g. on the board to emphasise the cue.)
4	*(Attention, John.)*	Walk over to John. Make sure he has the right page open. Point to the section on the page you are about to use.
5	*Un(e) volontaire, s'il vous plaît.*	This is a cognate in French which works.
6	*Merci. Viens ici.*	Beckon the volunteer to the front.
7	*Moi, je couvre la colonne B.*	Cover column B in your book with your hand. Show your volunteer what you have done and then show the class.
8	*Toi, mon partenaire, tu couvres la colonne A.*	Point to the learner's book column A and mime covering it over.
9	*La classe, regardez bien ... Une démonstration!*	Write the word 'demonstration' on the whiteboard. Look round and make sure everyone is watching.
10	*Tu commences ... (whisper ... pour une coupure:)*	Point to your partner to begin. Prompt with a stage whisper if required.
11	*(learner) Pour une coupure?*	Your volunteer partner speaks.
12	*(teacher again) Alors ... pour une coupure ... lavez la blessure avec du coton ...*	Make it obvious that you are looking for the reply from the list in the book and hold the book up to show where you have found it.

You will probably need to do two more examples before *'à vous maintenant!'*.

Example 2 (see note p38) follows the same techniques, this time for a freestanding activity. Each pair of learners has an envelope containing sets of cards. One set has pictures of people. The other set has matching descriptions.

	Words	Actions
1	*Regardez.*	Hold up the envelope containing the cards.
2	*Voilà des cartes.*	Take out the cards.
3	*Il y en a deux sortes.*	Hold up one pile in each hand.
4	*Voilà des images …*	Show the pile of picture cards.
5	*… et voilà des phrases.*	Show sentence cards.
6	(Time for a *'Faites attention'* here so they know it is the big moment of the explanation!) *Mettez les images comme ça.*	Show picture cards again and put them face down in a pile (worth repeating the action to stress that they should be face down).
7	*… et les phrases comme ça.* (Counting as you do it usefully fills in the silence while completing the action.)	Deal out sentence cards into three rows of four, face down.
8	*Je prends une carte … Ah, c'est une fille qui porte …*	Take the top card from the picture pile and comment on it.
9	*Je cherche … je choisis … voilà!*	Choose (with a touch of drama) a picture card from the spread.
10	*Elle porte un pantalon rouge.*	Hold up the sentence card (word side towards the class) and read it.
11	*C'est vrai – elle porte un pantalon? Oui. Rouge? Non. Alors, ce n'est pas vrai.*	Hold the two up together, repeating the phrase, looking backwards and forwards from one to the other.
12	*Alors je remets l'image SOUS les autres cartes …*	Replace the picture card UNDER the pile, making sure that UNDER is clear.
13	*Puis je remets la phrase.*	Replace the sentence card in its original position.

If we start with a skeletal framework of simple language like this, then we can fill it out as their (and our!) confidence and competence grows. For example:

$$\boxed{JETZT} \ldots \ldots \ldots \ldots \ldots \ldots \ldots \ldots \ldots \ldots \ldots \ldots \ldots \ldots \boxed{PARTNERARBEIT}$$

can become:

Also $\boxed{JETZT}$ *machen wir was anderes. Nun sollt ihr das mit euren* $\boxed{PARTNERN}$ *üben.*

The phrase *Also JETZT machen wir was anderes* can be developed as time goes on and in a systematic way, to:

- *Also jetzt machen wir **was neues***
- *Also jetzt machen wir **was verschiedenes***
- *Also jetzt machen wir **was schönes***

thus showing how language can be manipulated to alter meaning. It is also a way of illustrating grammatical features in use, before any kind of analysis or explanation. The same can be done with *Nun sollt ihr das mit euren PARTNERN üben.*

This can be developed as:

- *Nun **sollt ihr** das mit euren Partnern **schreiben***
- *Nun **sollt ihr** das mit euren Partnern **sprechen***
- *Nun **sollt ihr** mit euren Partnern die Aufgabe 2, auf Seite 101, **machen***

This question of our confidence in the approach is crucial. There is nothing inherently difficult in teaching in the target language. However, if either the teacher or the class is not used to it, it is the changeover which is difficult. We need strategies for carrying us through the temporary insecurities of change. This brings us to the second section.

Strategies for implementation

We offer these ideas under three headings:

- strategies for the teacher
- strategies for the learners
- strategies for the department as a whole

FOR THE INDIVIDUAL TEACHER

We each have a choice between: either   the 'slowly slowly' approach;
or   the 'it's now or never' approach.

If you prefer the 'slowly slowly' approach, we suggest the following.

Build up a repertoire of words and phrases

You could use the following headings as a guideline.

Instructions for classroom activities	
• *Bon, écoutez!*	• *Ecrivez …*
• *Faites un poster …*	• *Dessinez …*
• *Regardez!*	• *Remplissez la grille!*
• *Mimez …*	• *Couvrez …*
• *Trouvez la page xx*	• *Cochez votre grille!*
• *Copiez …*	• *Collez …*
• *Répétez!*	• *Vrai ou faux?*
• *Jouez …*	• *Choisissez …*
• *Lisez …*	• *Testez votre mémoire!*
• *Parlez plus fort/moins fort/ plus vite/moins vite*	• *Faites l'exercice (b), à la page xx*

Instructions for classroom organisation	
• *(Travaillez) avec un(e) partenaire*	• *Asseyez-vous! Assieds-toi!*
• *Echangez votre cahier …*	• *A vous maintenant*
• *(Travaillez) en groupes de quatre*	• *Dépêchez-vous! Dépêche-toi!*
• *Corrigez …*	
• *A tour de rôle*	

Change of activity markers	• *d'abord ...* • *alors ...* • *maintenant ...* • *pour terminer ...*
Nature of activity markers	• *question:* • *exemple:* • *réponse:*

Mild discipline exhortations	• *du calme, s'il vous plaît* • *faites comme ça* • *silence!* (said **softly**) • *tu as un problème?* • *ne fais/faites pas ça!*	(Beyond a certain point, however, these may not be effective. On occasions, it will make sense to suspend the language lesson and deal with the matter unequivocally in English.)
Expressing emotional reactions	• *Bravo!* • *(Très) bien* (as a reaction to the **message** and **not** to grammatical accuracy! (*Très bien* is, after all, a strange response to a pupil who answers a question such as: *Tu as des frères ou des sœurs?* with *Oui, j'ai un frère* and the reply is: *Ah, très bien!* More appropriate would be, perhaps; *Il s'appelle comment?*)) • *Bien dit!* • *Bonne prononciation!*	• *Bien écrit!* • *Bof!* • *Je n'aime pas ça!* • *Excellent!* • *Affreux!* (but avoid these applying to grammatical accuracy; they should be a response to the content/message, as mentioned before) • *Parfait!* • *Tu crois?* (example: learner says: *Il fait beau aujourd'hui*, you say: *Tu crois?*) • *Génial!*

Experiment with distinct blocks of target language talk

Do this rather than constantly switching between languages in a lesson. This can be backed up by:

• asking the learners to share the experimental nature of the enterprise. ('See how long we can keep going in Spanish'. 'I am going to do this bit all in Russian. If you get stuck, keep going and we will sort it out later'. A large egg timer can be useful here to count periods of three minutes.)

• explicitly practising phrases with them as a warm-up to a block of target language teaching.

It is only fair to point out that there can be a very real problem with the 'slowly slowly' approach. It is rather like doing income tax returns. There is always a very good reason for not doing it today:

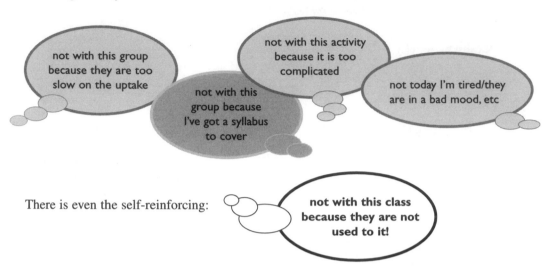

There is even the self-reinforcing:

not with this class because they are not used to it!

The danger here is that if we do not develop the strategies for the elements we find difficult, we will never do it. However, it is possible to combine some of the advantages of the two approaches. For example, it is feasible and sometimes more reassuring to:

- try it out with just one class first, preferably working with a colleague or with all members of the department. Choose the class you feel most comfortable with. But with that one class **go all out from Day One**.

- start with the next new intake and build target language use up through the school as those classes move up through it. In that sense it is 'slowly slowly'. But again with those classes go all out.

Finally, there is the question of grammar.

Here it may help in deciding what to do if we distinguish three main ways of teaching grammar. They are not mutually exclusive. Most of us use one or more of them. However, they each make slightly different demands on our use of the target language. By identifying which approach we are employing, we can identify the most sensible target language strategy for that approach. For example:

Approach 1 Letting the grammar emerge implicitly through the work. ➤ In this case we simply teach in the target language as suggested in earlier sections of this book.

Approach 2 Making the grammatical patterns visually and aurally explicit. ➤ In this case the board or the OHP is used to set out the pattern using different shapes, colours, blutack-ed endings, etc. Even something as simple as grouping vocabulary or structures as we write them up can help. We can then use the target language to draw attention to the visual pattern with additional key phrases like: *regardez la différence … Ça change … c'est important … Problem: … passt auf … nicht vergessen, etc.*

Approach 3   Discussing the grammar explicitly in grammatical terminology.➤ In this case we can either teach limited terminology in the target language and use that, and/or we can provide consolidating blocks of grammar work in English which are kept clearly separate from the rest of the work, probably most appropriate at ends of lessons or after periods of practice. As a result of the National Literacy Strategy in primary schools (DfEE 1998) (for application to the teaching and learning of MFL see DfES 2002) pupils should come into the secondary sector with greater grammatical understanding and the vocabulary with which to express it. This is our chance to benefit from their competence and to use target language equivalents to further learners' proficiency and even interest!

FOR THE LEARNERS

If the learners are to be encouraged to use the target language in return, then there will have to be ways of providing them with what they need. This has got to be quite deliberate and must be **'modelled'** by the teacher and built up systematically, preferably by all members of the Modern Languages department. For example, learners will need phrases in the target language for:

talking to you, e.g.

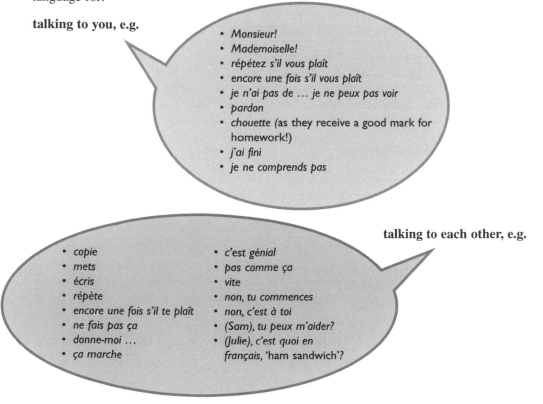

- *Monsieur!*
- *Mademoiselle!*
- *répétez s'il vous plaît*
- *encore une fois s'il vous plaît*
- *je n'ai pas de … je ne peux pas voir*
- *pardon*
- *chouette* (as they receive a good mark for homework!)
- *j'ai fini*
- *je ne comprends pas*

talking to each other, e.g.

- *copie*
- *mets*
- *écris*
- *répète*
- *encore une fois s'il te plaît*
- *ne fais pas ça*
- *donne-moi …*
- *ça marche*

- *c'est génial*
- *pas comme ça*
- *vite*
- *non, tu commences*
- *non, c'est à toi*
- *(Sam), tu peux m'aider?*
- *(Julie), c'est quoi en français, 'ham sandwich'?*

Just giving them a list to learn is unlikely to encourage them or to prove to be an easy task. Here are some other suggestions:

- As events occur in class (such as people absent when you take the register, hands up to leave the room, or a late entry), supply the target language phrase for what is needed. For example:

Er ist nicht hier. Er ist krank.
Puis-je quitter la salle?
Perdone me por llegar tarde.

- Similarly, give the learners the words in the target language that they have just used to show pleasure or an emotional reaction.

- During the lesson, as these words and phrases occur, write them on the whiteboard in a list to one side of the board. (It helps to have a 'scribble patch' where you can write 'extras' like this without getting in the way of the main work you are doing.) The words are then there as a reminder during the lesson and as the basis for a useful filler at the end of the lesson if you have a few minutes to spare. As has been suggested before, a list can also be written on an OHP transparency which grows quickly in length – often to the learners' surprise, because these are words they know and **use** all the time.

- Later, write these words and phrases on card. You can do this yourself or, better still, get some of the class to do so, perhaps in large print on the word processor in the ICT lesson. Pin the cards around the room (or even on the ceiling!). When needed they are then always there for reference.

- Introduce a new phrase and challenge the class to see how many times they can use it appropriately in the lesson. You can keep a running score in the scribble patch.

- Before setting up group or pairwork, deliberately practise some of the phrases they can use while they are doing the activity, e.g. *'Moment bitte!' 'Nicht gucken!' 'Los!'* Introduce one or two new ones and remind them of some they have already met. As well as practising how to say them, you can leave them up on the board or OHP as a prompt if required.

FOR THE DEPARTMENT

Whichever approach a teacher chooses, it is difficult working on one's own. It is much more helpful to have a policy for the whole department. Then the learners do not think they have the misfortune to have a teacher who sets out to make their life awkward. Teachers can also compare notes and support each other in the experiment. Here are some suggestions for departmental strategies:

- Have a departmental policy and keep to it.

- Work out an agreed starter list of language like the examples on pp24–25.

- If possible, go into each others' classrooms. Firstly, it is often much easier to see from the back of the room what could have been done. Secondly, someone else notices the errors that we ourselves miss when we are in full flow. Thirdly, there is nothing quite like having a colleague in the room to encourage one to make a success of something and really try!

• Decide as a department how to share with the learners what you are doing, what it involves for them and how it will help them.

• Decide as a department how to convey to the parents the approach to target language use and the thinking behind it. For example, some departments run demonstration events with the parents themselves as the class, or at parents' evenings, so that they can get the feel of what is involved.

• Hold some departmental workshops on INSET days.

The next section offers some ideas for these workshops.

3   Ideas for departmental workshops

The activities suggested here are intended as starting points and as a stimulus to developing ideas which suit the needs of your particular department. Most of them can be practised 'for real' on your own in the course of your daily teaching. However, practising teaching ideas on and with a small group of our colleagues has all kinds of advantages when we are working on improving existing techniques. Precisely because the event is not 'for real', we have the freedom to experiment and take risks without matters getting out of hand. We can laugh together over the things which do not quite work. We can stop and start again. We can produce an immediate revised version while the first attempt is still fresh in our minds. What is more, we have the advantage of having other people there who know what we are trying to do and can therefore give us explicit feedback of a kind which is missing from the classroom. We can also see in what others do a reflection of some of the things we ourselves do, both their advantages and disadvantages. We benefit from the additional ideas of other members of the department who may suggest things or spot problems we would never have thought of on our own. In turn, we can find ourselves stimulated to new ideas by what the others do. All too often we have little opportunity to learn from and with each other in this way once we leave our initial training. The ideas which follow offer a chance to do just that. They focus in different ways on:

- making the most of the non-language messages;
- learning to keep the language initially simple, but then planning a systematic grammatical development;
- setting up work in stages by showing and doing.

Suggestion 1	**To practise conveying simple classroom instructions by gesture, mime and example**

You could each write on strips of paper several of the instructions you would expect to have to issue in a language class. Put all of the strips into a bag or box. Take it in turns to pick out a strip 'blind' and **without saying anything at all** 'instruct' the others in the group to do it. If necessary, concentrate on breaking down the instructions into stages.

pack away everything off the desks

put your chairs up on the desk

work with a partner

write the date on a clean page in the fron of your exercise books

<table>
<tr><td>Suggestion 2</td><td>To practise showing how to do something</td></tr>
</table>

You could each choose in advance something which you can teach the others to make, e.g. a paper 'Fortune Teller' or a paper model or a chocolate truffle. Show them how to do it stage by stage, **still without saying anything.**

<table>
<tr><td>Suggestion 3</td><td>To identify a core of simple phrases and words</td></tr>
</table>

You could start by collecting and sharing a basic list of marker phrases, signal words, cues and all-purpose phrases you are likely to need (see pp24–25 for some guideline headings). If there is a Foreign Language Assistant in school, he or she will be invaluable here. They too will benefit from thinking of the simplest version.

<table>
<tr><td>Suggestion 4</td><td>To identify a simple core of words for the learners</td></tr>
</table>

You could agree on the content of, and each design, an initial *'pour vous aider'* board, wall posters or 'inspiration clouds' which the learners consult when in difficulty.

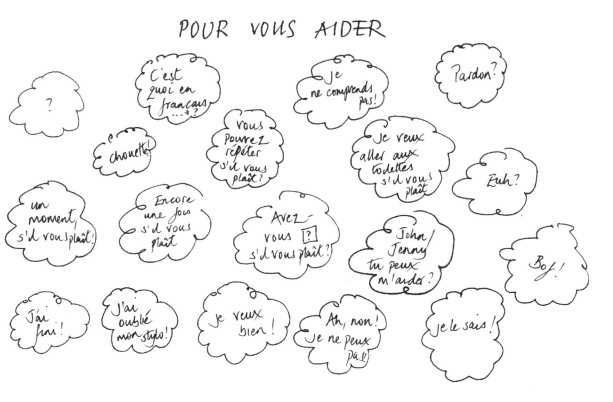

LIVERPOOL ... TY COLLEGE

Suggestion 5	To practise keeping language initially simple

You could agree to restrict yourselves to a **limited** number of phrases (e.g. *Ecoutez, regardez, faites comme ça* + a free choice of three more) and use those few phrases to back up the kind of demonstration as indicated under Suggestion 2, e.g. teach the others how to make a 'Fortune Teller'.

Suggestion 6	Another activity to practise keeping language simple

You could each choose a language of which you know only very little or get someone else in the department to teach you a limited number of phrases as in Suggestion 4. Then take it in turns to use mime, gesture, drawing, OHP and example backed by those few phrases to set up one of the previous activities.

Suggestion 7	To identify and extend the range of possible ways of 'telling' by showing

You could choose an activity which is common to all of you or taken from the textbook you use and take it in turns to set the activity up using a different method of showing, e.g.

- one concentrates on using the OHP;
- one uses flashcards (words or pictures);
- one uses only the whiteboard;
- one uses real objects;
- one uses only the textbook or a leaflet.

Compare the effect of each of these and discuss ways of combining them.

Suggestion 8	To practise setting activities up stage by stage

You could make a list of some of the activities most common in your teaching materials, e.g. introducing a listening comprehension, setting up oral pairwork based on picture prompts, launching a class *sondage,* playing a memory game, requiring a written exercise. Take it in turns to set up one of them using all the techniques of 'telling by showing' and limited phrases. This time concentrate on setting the event by **doing** each stage **with** the 'class'.

Suggestion 9	To compare the advantages of different ways of introducing activities

You could agree on one common but fairly complex activity you are all likely to introduce at some stage, e.g. 'battleships' or a class survey grid. In advance, each prepare independently a way of explaining by showing and doing in stages and compare the effectiveness of the different approaches in conveying the meaning alongside the language. Try to draw out any generalisable principles.

Suggestion 10	To practise highlighting grammar pattern visually

You could each choose in advance a particular grammar pattern, e.g. the relative clause in German, the preterite in Spanish, the partitive in French, and take it in turns to build that pattern up on the board and OHP using a few general target language comments to highlight the crucial points (see Approach 3 p27). If you can do this in a language that some of your colleagues do not share, then all to the good.

Suggestion 11	To practise discussing grammar in the target language

You could jointly make a list of a few key grammatical terms in the target language and then repeat Suggestion 10 with these few terms added. The National Literacy Strategy provides helpful lists.

Suggestion 12	To practise making unavoidable English as indirect as possible

You could each choose a genuine homework task which perhaps you would normally have set in English; practise keeping your own target language going but giving essential clues in English (notes, keywords, summary, etc) on the whiteboard as you speak. Even if the clues are temporarily in English, the class will have heard them in the target language. Check by using a class interpreter that the instructions have really been understood.

Suggestion 13	To explore how initially simple target language can be extended systematically

You could, as a department, choose any of the language phrases you have listed under Suggestions 3 and 4. Explore how any of these can be extended systematically over time:

Examples – say **first** what is shown in Column 1 and **add** the extension shown in Column 2.

Column One Original version	Column Two Extension added to the original
Je ne comprends pas	*Je n'ai pas compris*
Ecrivez!	*Voulez-vous écrire, s'il vous plaît ...*
Répétez!	*Voulez-vous répéter, s'il vous plaît ...*
Dessinez!	*Voulez-vous dessiner s'il vous plaît ...*
Parlez plus fort!	*Voulez-vous parler plus fort, s'il vous plaît*

Fini!	*J'ai fini! C'est fait! Ça y est!*
Je n'ai pas de cahier	*Mon cahier? Je l'ai oublié*
Je n'ai pas de stylo	*Mon stylo? Je l'ai oublié*
J'ai oublié mon stylo	*Désolé*
Ah, non. Impossible!	*Je ne peux pas!*
Encore une fois, s'il vous plaît?	*Vous pouvez répéter, encore une fois, s'il vous plaît?*

SOME GENERAL POINTS

• If you can, bring in a native speaker to help with these activities. This helps the department linguistically, gives the assistant the boost of a key role to play and, equally importantly, shows the assistant strategies she or he will need for teaching in the native tongue.

• If you have a departmental video camera, why not video yourselves doing some of these activities?

• See if you can persuade some colleagues from other subject departments to join you to provide a 'class'. If they don't speak very much of the target language, all the better. In fact, we should also not forget that our science colleagues, in particular, are very familiar with the ideas and techniques of explaining by showing and will have ideas to offer.

• If you are a very small department, some of the ideas as they appear above would be difficult to set up. Schools often have their INSET days on the same day. If you cannot find colleagues from other subjects willing to act as guinea pigs, why not see if you could join forces with language colleagues from another school for the day?

• If you have recent entrants to the profession in the department, or PGCE students placed in the school on teaching practice, it will be worth asking them for ideas, examples and demonstrations. All of them will have been encouraged to teach in the target language from the start. It will also help them to discover that they have expertise to offer as well as so much to learn.

4 Troubleshooting

YES, BUT WHAT IF ...

They reply in English to what we say in the target language

This can happen for several reasons:

a They may want to annoy or provoke or try to be awkward by not 'playing the game'. If so, it is probably best to ignore their reaction and continue, in a simple version of the target language.

b They can be genuinely lost. If this happens, rephrase what you have just been saying in the target language, e.g.

> you: *Jetzt macht ihr das mit eurem Partner oder mit eurer Partnerin, bis einer von euch gewonnen hat. Und dann umtauschen!*
> them: You mean we swap over ...?
> you: *Ja! Wenn einer gewonnen hat, tauscht ihr um.* (+ mime)

Or failing this you can ask one member of the group to be *Dolmetscher/interprète*: '*Peter. Sag das bitte auf Englisch.*' At least here you stay in the foreign language, while someone else's English reassures or clarifies.

c They are being lazy. You know your class. This might be a moment to insist.

They produce a mixture of the target language and English

If they are willing to do this, we are more than half way there, so continue to react as if it had all been in the foreign language. If you believe the English was only a momentary substitute for a lost or forgotten word or phrase, supply this as part of a natural response in the foreign language.

They make mistakes

They are bound to make mistakes and need to do so, if what they are doing is concentrating on conveying meaning, rather than being over-concerned with correct linguistic form. Again, in as natural a way as possible, rephrase their statement or response in an appropriately correct version of their original.

They talk to each other in English

Sometimes this is inevitable. However, it is always worth asking ourselves whether we have taught them the target language versions of what they come out with in English. If not, then the responsibility lies with us and not with them! If the reason seems to be a lack of motivation or willingness, try appointing one of the pupils in a partner activity as *le juge linguistique* who says *'Répète en français, s'il te plaît'/'Sag das bitte auf Deutsch'*, or who, in a class activity, says (using one of a set of agreed formulae), *'C'est quoi en français?'/'Wie sagt man das auf Deutsch?'*

You are in the middle of explaining and they become impatient and say 'What's all that in English?'

Try to add as many helpful visual explanations of the language as possible (using coloured pens, chalks, different shapes, letters on card blutack-ed to the board), e.g.

words written in drywipe pen on the board   *Sharon s'est levé* | *e* | letter on card blutack-ed to the board

Then (after, in this example, changing the name before the verb) ask one of the class to come out and select the correct letter from a pile on the teacher's table, e.g.

Elle a mis une jupe | *vert* | *e* | | *bleu* | *e* | | *orange* |

Again, ask members of the class to come out and make up their jigsaw pieces into, say, appropriate captions for a series of magazine photos.

You can always encourage an interpreter to explain in English the pattern which you have been trying to illustrate. Sometimes an individual's version of what's going on can be clearer than anything that you have said in any language!

You have made a mistake

	*Zut! C'est **un** parapluie.*
	J'écris ça pour vous aider: un parapluie.
(cover *'un'*)	*Toi, Georges, répète ...!*
Georges:	*Un parapluie.*
	Georges est très intelligent, n'est-ce pas?

They want to interrupt and translate

Say: *'Oui, c'est bien ça'* if they are correct. *'Non, c'est faux'* if they are incorrect. Then give an appropriately rephrased version of what you were saying in the foreign language.

You could save an awful lot of time by saying something in English

Do so, if it is only one word. (Think how many times you do this in the foreign language when speaking English to a French or German native speaker.) Better to sustain your message with one word whispered in English than to spend five minutes swinging from the chandeliers trying to mime *'faire la culbute'* (to somersault).

If, however, you 'give in' for anything longer or more complex, then you are doing your class and yourself a disservice. Perhaps you have not been:

a simplifying sufficiently;

b backing up your oral instructions or explanations with numbered and staged instructions in the target language, written on the board as you speak;

c using key words on the board which have English equivalent lookalikes or quick sketches to exemplify meaning.

You have a new child in the class who does not understand

a Use the interpreter technique with someone from the class who has befriended the newcomer.

b See if any of the class can explain something in the target language.

c Spend time during the lesson, when the class is doing something independently of you, explaining how you give explanations or set activities in the target language and what sort of language you use to do this. If you have already written many of these on cards displayed around the room, ask one of the class to explain what is there.

They just dismiss the whole process as stupid

Do not give up! Try a timed *'x minutes en français', 'x Minuten auf Deutsch!'* on the next occasion you see them. Set yourself, and them, limited targets. Congratulate them afterwards! *'Bien! 10 minutes en français'* – *'Schön, 10 Minuten auf Deutsch! Prima!'* See if, next lesson, they can beat their record.

Finally, in practising these approaches we must not lose sight of why we are doing it, or they just become inflexible and even burdensome rituals. This brings us back to the starting point of Part 1.

We are teaching in the target language in order to give our learners a better chance of learning another language effectively. We are:

• making the language a real tool that they experience in use;
• giving them the confidence to get by when they emerge from the protection of the classroom;
• above all providing another very powerful channel of learning the language itself.

Bibliography

DfEE (1998) *The National Literacy Strategy: framework for teaching*. Department for Education and Employment Publications.

DfEE (1999) *Modern Foreign Languages: The National Curriculum for England*. Department for Education and Employment and Qualifications and Curriculum Authority.

DfES (2002) *Key Stage 3 National Literacy Strategy in Modern Foreign Languages*. Department for Education and Skills.

Harris V., Burch J., Jones B., and Darcy J. (2001) *Something to say? Promoting spontaneous classroom talk*. CILT.

Note: the extract on p22 is from an article (under Susan Halliwell's former name of Susan Maclennan) in *NALA Journal 18,* July 1987.

Part 2

Keeping
on target

BERNARDETTE HOLMES

Introduction: recognising the extent of the challenge

Picture the scene – a temporary classroom at the back of the science block, a damp September, Friday afternoon last period, following a PE lesson and there they are, our new Year 10 German group. They have all had opportunities to study German and French from 11 to 14 but have chosen to continue German up to examination. Some of them come from the same teaching group as last year, but, because the option blocks are arranged as they are, there are others who come from different groups and one or two who are new to the school altogether. There are also a few from that group that have had three different teachers during Year 9 for various reasons. Let us meet them!

The cognitive analytical learner

There is Rebecca – keen, able, high achieving, participated in the German exchange in Year 9, regular contributor to class e-mail link with Germany, confident in listening, reading and writing, but even after the German exchange visit, will she use the target language for all classroom communication? Not until she has checked every word in the dictionary and consulted a grammar table, she won't!

Challenge!   To encourage the cognitive analytical learner to take risks.

The communicative interactive learner

That would be Jack – always inaccurate, but very willing to have a go. He'll say anything to get his meaning across. To be fair, he is very good at memorising stock phrases, but he doesn't seem to be able to adapt them to new contexts.

Challenge!   To provide the necessary support for Jack to develop more analytical competence, perhaps by pairing him with a more cognitive analytical learner, like Rebecca.

The divergent introvert

Then there is Nasser – very quiet, doesn't seem to be participating in whole-class activities, likes to do things his own way, but some of his creative writing is really promising. He is trying to experiment with language and make new meanings, even if it wasn't exactly what he was supposed to be doing!

Challenge! To help Nasser plan his learning and use his creativity more strategically.

The convergent extrovert

This would be Callum! If you want someone to participate in any class game or quiz, he is the man! Providing he is given clear objectives and sufficient support, he is manageable. Of course, if you are not careful, as he never stops talking, most of his contributions will be in English.

Challenge! Make sure Callum is engaged from the moment he enters the classroom. Give him really clear instructions and keep him active.

The divergent extrovert

This is Tomaz – he will not do things your way and it is not just a question of non-co-operation; he is noisy and distracts the rest. The only positive influence on him is what Callum thinks about him. Get Callum on side and it is likely that Tomaz will follow.

Challenge! Keep Callum on side.

The convergent introvert

That must be Cleo – very quiet, very co-operative, presents her work well and is very able to communicate both in speech and writing, if she is not placed in a stressful learning environment. If we are not careful, she can become almost invisible in the classroom.

Challenge! Make sure Cleo builds self-confidence! Give her plenty of opportunity to work in pairs or small groups, where she has a defined role and can develop her ideas with the support of her peers. In this way, she can take an active part without feeling under pressure to perform.

If we take **keeping on target** to mean the consistent use of the target language for the business of all classroom communication, then it presents certain challenges for both teachers and learners. This part of the book is an attempt to provide insights into the nature of those challenges and propose some strategies in order to address them.

There are various factors which affect progression in using the target language. Some of these we can control; some we can't.

Prior learning can leave a less than positive legacy in relation to pupils' willingness to use the target language and accept it as the normal means of communication. There may be changes of teacher, changes of group, changes in the choice of language studied which mean that our learners may have had a very mixed experience of teaching methods and approaches to the use of the target language. We may need to rebuild the foundations in order to make further progress.

Lack of motivation is arguably the most serious barrier to progression. If our pupils see little value in learning a foreign language, then we will have to find ways of changing their attitudes. Finding suitable contexts for learning which create the need and desire to communicate will be a key issue.

Differences in learning styles represent another dimension to this challenge. Rebecca, Jack, Nasser, Callum, Tomaz and Cleo all have different learning needs. A 'one-size-fits-all' approach to teaching will not be sufficient to support them and provide an appropriate structure for progression in their learning. It will be in everyone's best interest to provide a range of learning opportunities for individuals, pairs and groups, which offers balance between active, experiential learning and more reflective, formal activities.

Assessing the baseline is the first step in planning an appropriate learning programme to promote pupil use of the target language. What can the majority of learners do so far? OFSTED findings tell us that most learners generally respond positively to whole-class chorus work, when defined content is presented and rehearsed in a variety of ways. Short exchanges in pairs are conducted well, but opportunities to communicate at any length in either speech or writing are more limited. Learners rarely take the initiative or use language spontaneously in new contexts.

Is this reluctance to experiment with language brought about by fear of making mistakes or through lack of motivation? What can we do to encourage spontaneity? How can we support them to step beyond the basic response?

Progression: stepping beyond the basic response

'A word devoid of thought is a dead thing and a thought unembodied in words remains a shadow.' Vygotsky

- Learning is motivated by our desire to make sense of the world.
- Learning is a cognitive process.
- Learning comes through social and cultural interaction.
- We learn through language.
- We need language to make sense of the world.
- Progression is a feature of effective learning.

If we accept these notions of learning, there are implications for planning for progression. We have to make the link between language and thought, language and learning. This has implications for the content and process of our teaching.

Progression in language learning will hinge on the volition, motivation and determination of our learners to communicate in the target language. We have to give them something worthwhile to talk about or why would they want to say anything anyway?

If we think about the Piagetian stages of cognitive development, this period of adolescence from eleven years onwards is characterised by the ability to think logically about abstract propositions and test hypotheses systematically. It is at this Formal Operational stage that pupils become concerned about the future, seek to address ideological problems and become more pre-occupied with the hypothetical. It is unsurprising that much of the content of the MFL curriculum fails to sustain their interest.

This is part of the dilemma for teachers of foreign languages. As Hawkins (1987) reminds us:

> *'The infant acquiring the mother tongue is, at the same time, making a series of exciting discoveries about the world [...] These discoveries once made cannot be unlearnt.'*

A challenge for us will be to make the language-learning curriculum more cognitively challenging.

Rich and stimulating input

We could address this challenge by providing a range of learning opportunities which, as well as serving to increase their knowledge and understanding about the foreign language itself, also contribute to what they learn through language in relation to their personal growth and development as individuals.

Learning about language and through language are not incompatible processes. Here is an example of a simple poem that has been used to promote understanding about adjectives and adjectival agreement, while raising awareness of citizenship and the multicultural world in which we live:

> **Ton Christ est juif.**
>
> **Ta voiture est japonaise,**
>
> **ta pizza est italienne et ton couscous algérien.**
>
> **Ta démocratie est grecque.**
>
> **Ton café est brésilien,**
>
> **ta montre est suisse, ta chemise est indienne,**
>
> **et ta radio est coréenne,**
>
> **tes vacances sont turques, tunisiennes ou marocaines.**
>
> **Tes chiffres sont arabes, ton écriture est latine.**
>
> **Et ... tu reproches à ton voisin d'être un étranger.**

Learners are encouraged to focus on both the form and content of the poem, finding out about language and how it works, but also reflecting on the power of language to shape our thoughts and attitudes. The follow-up activity to the poem is to write a personal response either as an alternative last line, a thought bubble or a new verse.

Learners tend to make greater progress in both spoken and written communication if they are offered opportunities to invest something of themselves into their learning. Activities must be perceived as relevant. Conceptual bridges should be built between the known and the unknown, while offering opportunities to compare and contrast the self with others. It will not be enough for the secondary age group to simply rename things that they know already in English, unless we give them an appropriate context in which to do so.

The inspiring cross-curricular project carried out by the Blackheath Bluecoat School in South-East London provides just such a context. The school took part in the 'On the line' project, run by Oxfam, Channel 4 and WWF (World Wildlife Fund), which explored the lives of people living along the Greenwich Meridian Line at the turn of the millennium, linking people and places in eight countries, including some of the richest and poorest countries on the planet. The school developed a link with another school in Burkina Faso, West Africa, and set up a comparative study of lifestyles and cultures. This involved virtual and real contacts between young people, exploring similarities and differences and fostering a positive response to 'otherness'. Elements of CLIL (Content and Language Integrated Learning) were developed, with part of the NC Programmes of Study for Geography and Citizenship delivered through the medium of French. (This example is courtesy of Neil Jones, now working at Elliot School, Putney.)

Using the here and now

The power of social interaction to stimulate learning and promote progression cannot be underestimated. Using the target language for real purposes in the here and now rather than as a rehearsal for encounters that may never happen should occupy a central role in our planning. It is not always possible to set up face-to-face communication with speakers of the target language, but the more we can embed ICT into our teaching to allow virtual contacts, 'e' pals, shared websites, videoconferencing, the better.

There are also messages about the language-learning process within the classroom and the development of pupil-to-pupil use of the target language. In curriculum planning this area of target language tends to be underdeveloped and yet it is in this area that the most progress can be made over time. We need to develop an ethos where genuine interaction between pupils is the focus of our lessons and where it is expected that learners will talk to one another formally in teacher-led situations and informally as they carry out the business of learning.

Why is it important to promote pupil-to-pupil use of the target language?

The most persuasive reason is that unless we can maximise exposure to the target language by our sustained use of it and the pupils' willingness to use it, where else are they likely to experience the language? As Professor Hawkins describes in his powerful image of 'gardening in a gale', we are surrounded by English and for most learners the classroom will be their only encounter with the foreign language. So, we will need to structure that experience in order to accelerate their learning and enable them to internalise familiar language and re-use it for their own purposes.

Unlike first-language acquisition, second-language learning in anything other than a bilingual environment is likely to be a more deliberate and conscious process. Our aim, as teachers, will be to provide appropriate learning opportunities in order to make the use of the target language by our pupils increasingly more natural and spontaneous. We will attempt to do this by developing activities for two different but complementary purposes: activities which help them to use language communicatively to convey their thoughts and feelings; and activities which help them to learn about language and language-learning strategies.

> *'Second language learning in formal contexts is an intentional process whose success depends on the gradual automatisation of tasks that are first performed with a high degree of conscious intention and control.'*

There are two fundamental implications for our teaching:

i. *'We must accord a central role to use of the target language, otherwise learners cannot be expected to develop even a limited capacity for automatic processing.*

ii *We must adopt an explicitly reflective approach to the conduct of classroom activities, whether their principal focus is language learning or language use.'*

(Little 1999)

WHAT IS COMMUNICATIVE COMPETENCE AND HOW DO WE MONITOR LINGUISTIC PROGRESSION?

(Canale 1983)

Attempts to define communicative competence began with Canale and Swain in 1980 and a further refinement by Canale in 1983. The definition focuses on four components: grammatical, strategic, socio-linguistic and discourse competence. If we take each of these in turn, we can firstly explore their relevance and what they might mean for teaching and learning in the classroom, and secondly, we can investigate their value in relation to mapping the progression of our hypothetical learners, Rebecca, Jack, Nasser, Callum, Tomaz and Cleo.

Grammatical competence

This is defined in terms of breadth of lexis, awareness of syntax and structure. It can exist and be studied in a decontextualised form (e.g.verb tables). Rules can be memorised and tested. However, there is little research evidence to suggest that knowledge about language studied in isolation has any positive impact on accelerating progression.

A performance indicator of grammatical competence is whether Rebecca, the cognitive analytical learner, has sufficient confidence to express an action that took place yesterday, using the perfect tense without checking first in the verb table. Does Jack, the communicative interactive learner, have enough awareness of grammatical pattern to be able to modify a stock phrase and transfer language to new contexts?

grammar

Internalising
a language system
to enable independence

Johnstone (CILT Grammar conference)

The usage of the term 'grammar' can cause some problems. Susan Halliwell puts forward some helpful definitions for us:

- Grammar as description – Do we mean what language conveys in terms of general notions and functions?

- Grammar as terminology – Do we mean the terms that we use, e.g. past anterior, preceding direct object, adverb, noun?

- Grammar as rules – Do we mean descriptive codification of the inner workings of the language, telling us what we have to do to make up particular language forms, e.g. you make the future tense of regular verbs in -er and -ir by taking the infinitive and adding the endings -ai, -as, -a, -ons, -ez, -ont?

- Grammar as pattern – Do we mean recognising language patterns, e.g. *mit dem Bus, mit dem Auto, mit dem Flugzeug **aber** mit der Straßenbahn*? Learner-friendly definitions of grammar, where we encourage the learners to spot the difference and suggest the rules for themselves (Halliwell, 1993).

Strategic competence

This is all to do with linguistic problem-solving, dealing with the unpredictable. What do you do when your existing knowledge of language runs out? Once communication extends beyond defined, rehearsed content, how can you convey a message and stretch your linguistic resources?

The original definition suggests that strategic competence only applies when we need to compensate for breakdowns in communication, but more recently, as David Little points out, strategic competence has been thought of as a more pro-active and positive process. He describes strategic competence as being 'offensive' rather than 'defensive', referring to Bachman's definition:

> *Strategic competence has three components: assessment, planning and execution which comprise a set of meta-cognitive processes, or strategies which can be thought of as higher-order executive processes that provide a cognitive management function in language use, as well as other cognitive activities.*

> (Bachman 1990 and Bachman and Palmer 1996)

Here we would include second-language learning. So, we can take it that strategic competence is not just about bailing us out when we are failing, but more about helping us to communicate more effectively. In these terms, strategic competence occupies a central function in all aspects of learning.

In the language classroom we could be talking about developing communication strategies which combine words and non-verbal communication like mime or gesture, repair strategies like rephrasing or repeating for clarification, using paraphrase, creating metaphors. Here we are very close to the realm of creativity and imagination.

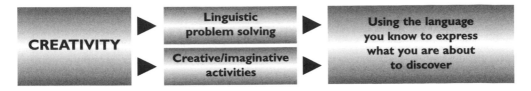

We can extend the definition of strategic competence to include the way learners plan their learning and approach a task. We could also include their use of reference materials, dictionaries, vocabulary books and simple verbal requests for help and clarification in the target language.

Success in this dimension would see Cleo, the convergent introvert, communicating more readily perhaps, as greater development of strategic competence would certainly reduce the stress in more spontaneous, open-ended speech acts.

Socio-linguistic competence

Developing socio-linguistic competence means being able to interpret the language you use according to the situation and social context in which you find yourself. It is about matching the rules to real purposes appropriately, following conventions of time, place and person. It embraces language functions like greetings, requests, explanations, agreeing and disagreeing, politeness phrases.

So, thinking about communicating with native speakers, can Callum use the appropriate register to speak to an adult visitor from abroad? Has he got 'street cred' when talking to his exchange partner?

Turning our attention to the here and now of the classroom, socio-linguistic competence is what it's all about! Using the target language for real in the classroom provides opportunities for genuine communication of all kinds.

Can Callum persuade his partner to lend him a pen? Can Rebecca encourage Callum and Tomaz to work quietly! Can they give each other instructions during a role-play? Can they express how fed up they are with someone cheating in the dice game?

Discourse competence

This involves more sustained communication which builds on ideas and may involve a number of different topics. Success is measured by the learners' ability to cope with internal structuring, taking the initiative, introducing fresh ideas logically into a conversation or discussion, sequencing ideas coherently and changing topic appropriately. It can be exemplified when learners are required to justify their thinking, hold a multi-person discussion in a group activity, or present information cohesively in a structured talk.

In relation to written communication, there are familiar conventional text types. What tells you that something is a letter, or a play script, a newspaper article, a menu, a poem, a conversation in a novel?

Thinking back to our hypothetical learners, this is another area which is most probably underdeveloped and yet it is essential if we are to succeed in enabling learners to say what they want to say. There will need to be very specific stages built into activities to allow for the development of discourse competence. We will need to provide an appropriate scaffold to support progression. This could come in the form of differentiated materials and levels of support or in the way we use pair and group work. However we choose to address this, it will imply strategic planning over time.

All four dimensions of communicative competence will have an impact on learners' confidence, capability and willingness to use the target language for their own purposes. There is much more to keeping on target than would at first appear.

independence

Taking control of your use and response to language

Linguistic management

Johnstone (CILT Grammar conference)

THE NATURE OF CHALLENGE

Progression could be described as a function of challenge. Learning is frequently described as ineffective where activities offer insufficient challenge. The meaning of challenge in this context is often left undefined. Let us consider here that it relates to levels of linguistic and cognitive demand. In both of these aspects the nature and purpose of questioning have a part to play.

Effective questioning

We often use quick-fire questioning as a device for revising and consolidating items of vocabulary or short single-function sentences. This is a perfectly valid activity for developing progression at word level or to rehearse set-piece phrases, 'chunks of language'.

Questions used for this kind of activity are usually closed – they have only one possible answer. They involve a low level of factual recall and do not place excessive cognitive demands upon the learner, largely because the concepts that they represent are not newly discovered. Such questions make a very limited contribution to promoting deeper understanding or the ability to manipulate language to make new meanings. In this respect they are less valuable in developing the broader purpose of communication, which should embrace choice of response and may involve the expression of thoughts, feelings and opinions. But then, such questioning is not intended to serve this purpose. It is about building vocabulary and is a necessary part of language learning. There are other parts which are perhaps, as yet, under developed.

There could, for example, be greater emphasis on a balance between closed quick-fire questioning and open-ended, probing questioning, which is more thought provoking. If this is so, there needs to be a necessary shift in the management of class questioning.

Extensive research in Western Australia in primary education reported that teachers ask questions at an average rate of one every twelve seconds (evidence has been taken from a five-year longitudinal study, the Language and Learning Project 1977–1982, conducted by the Western Australian Education Department). There is a wait time of only one second before a response from the learners is expected! Lessons could be learned here in relation to the foreign languages classroom and our quest to develop higher-order language outcomes and greater independence. If we ask more demanding questions, we could deliberately leave time for the students to develop their ideas and refine their response. We may wish to build in opportunities to use reference materials or consult with a partner or small group.

Providing adequate **wait time** could be a very simple but effective way of moving learners on to produce more thoughtful answers, comments or opinions. In addition, this could create a more reflective environment for the classroom where thinking time and purposeful talk in the target language become part of the culture.

Developing thinking skills

Challenge in relation to the nature of tasks usually relates to the cognitive demands made by the activity. Language is a cognitive process. Activities which rely on low levels of thinking tend to produce low levels of language contribution.

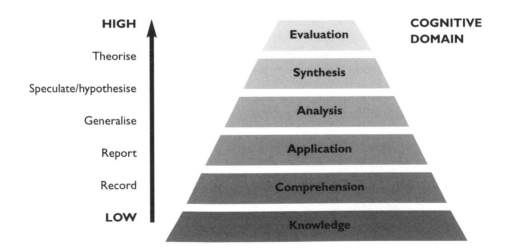

Theories about cognitive challenge often refer to Bloom's Taxonomy which, though not the only system to be devised, is still widely used. In it Bloom sought to classify forms of learning within the behavioural paradigm. Bloom suggested that 'knowing the facts' is at the lowest level in the cognitive domain. He defines a structure for cognitive development, which attempts to divide cognitive objectives into a sequence of progressive stages ranging from the simplest to the most complex behaviour, as the learner interacts with information and puts it in context. Each stage subsumes the previous stages.

We can increase the level of linguistic and cognitive demand by very simple adjustments to activities. For example, in a matching activity where Christmas presents are linked to a family group whose description is provided, why not remove the family description and ask our learners to look at the presents that have been bought and conjecture as to what kind of a family you think this person may have. We are then entering the world of speculation and hypothesis.

Varying the model for learning

Enhanced challenge can also come through the way we organise or contrive the learning situation. The most commonly used model for learning is teacher presentation, whole-class practice, followed by further practice in pairs and less often groups. We may find that use of the target language by pupils will increase if we are willing to take risks with the model and use more flexible approaches to whole-class learning. There can be a healthy balance between activities which have a kick start by teacher stimulus and demonstration and those which begin with the learners' ideas, perhaps through individual, to pair, to group processes or brainstorming.

There can be rich rewards in terms of the quality and range of language used if group work is managed more creatively. Again, drawing on work developed initially in Western Australia, we can investigate the value of using small group work, with a focus on home groups and reconfigured groups. This approach is illustrated in Figure A. Learners can have an individual responsibility to a home group, where they express their ideas and explore the ideas of others. Opportunities are given to reshape information and reformulate ideas and language forms. The role of the teacher and Foreign Language Assistant is to support and extend the language used by sensitive intervention. Small group work allows learners to accelerate their learning through social interaction with their peers.

The learners then combine in reconfigured groups (Figure B), where they present and share results of their activities. There is further reshaping, collaboration and creative activity. Learners then return to the home groups and present their finished work in the target language as much as possible.

Each transition to the learning can be supported by a whole-class plenary discussion, where the teacher or learners can share examples of good practice, explain difficulties, reformulate ideas and promote progression. Such discussions provide opportunities for learners to reflect on what they have learnt so far, how they are learning and how they could learn better.

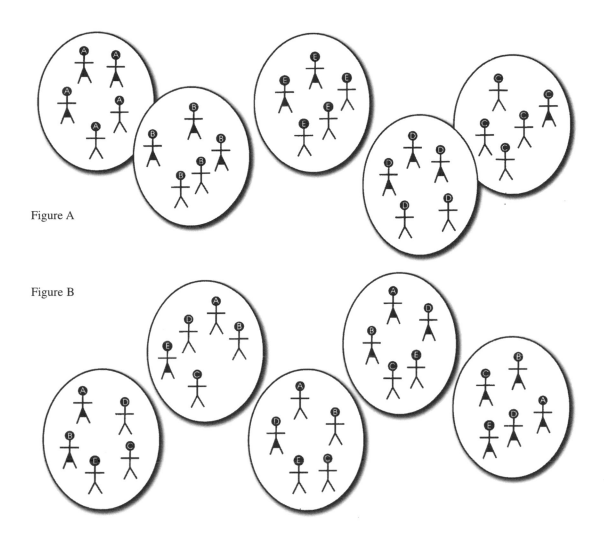

Figure A

Figure B

The foundation of defined content is radically shaken by such approaches. There will be a core of language, identified by the teacher or coursebook, which is to be included in an activity and explicitly taught. But through the process of creative group work, the core will be extended differently according to the language needs of the learners. The agenda for learning is their own. They are saying what they want to say.

Opportunities where pupils of different abilities and learning styles work together and learn from one another is one of the key notions in Vygotsky's approach to cognitive development: **the zone of proximal development.**

> *The distance between the actual developmental level as determined by independent problem solving and the level of potential development as determined through problem solving under adult guidance or in collaboration with more capable peers.*

(Vygotsky 1978 edition)

Through the social context of pair and group interaction the learners can model and extend what they say and in so doing, improve the quality of their thinking skills. If we can extend this theory to foreign language learning, the communicative classroom that operates through the target language should raise the standards of all learners by virtue of shared learning.

The teacher or 'expert adult' has a crucial role in setting up support structures or **scaffolding** (Wood, Bruner and Ross 1976) to enable learners to improve their linguistic and cognitive skills. As learners' confidence increases, the layers of scaffolding can gradually be removed to ensure that the learners make progress.

WHERE ARE WE SO FAR?

We have thought about progression, the centrality of finding stimulating content, the importance of social interaction in the here and now and the different strands involved in developing communicative competence. We have taken a closer look at the nature of challenge and what it might mean in terms of our role in the classroom, the way we use questioning and the definition of challenging tasks. We have begun to consider how language tasks might contribute to developing thinking skills.

In terms of the process of language learning to promote progression …

- there will need to be a balance between individual, pair and group work;
- whole-class teacher-led activities will still be very relevant but may need to evolve and take account of learners' ideas to a greater extent and involve discussion about learning strategies;
- emphasis should be given to the quality of interaction between pupils using the target language to communicate with one another;
- compensation strategies which enable learners to cope with making sense of unfamiliar language when they are not in control should be developed;
- repair strategies such as rephrasing or repeating for clarification can be fostered;
- communication strategies can be encouraged, like non-verbal communication and paraphrase;
- a wider range of communication can be expected – transactional exchanges, conversations, presentations and structured talks, discussion and argumentation;
- there can be a greater focus on grammatical awareness and reference skills.

In order to progress, learners must move on from the cycle of recognition and response/ imitation and production of unanalysed chunks of language. They will need to develop a range of more complex linguistic and social skills. If they are to become independent users of the target language, we will need to provide them with opportunities to adapt language to new circumstances and learn how to negotiate, describe, explain, persuade. We must support them in developing grammatical, strategic, socio-linguistic and discourse competence.

Time, perhaps, to open the classroom door and take a look at some teaching and learning activities and consider what kind of contribution they can make to progression.

2 Through the keyhole: a glimpse at classroom practice

Here are some reflections on activities which have been developed in the classroom with real rather than hypothetical learners. They range from activities which concentrate on sound to activities which promote more extended use of language.

BREAKING THE SOUND BARRIER

Often learners' reluctance to use language more spontaneously is a result of lack of confidence. Perhaps they know and can respond to a range of classroom language but are unwilling to adapt and transfer such language to active use because the words are difficult to pronounce. Maybe there was some difficulty in discriminating between the different sounds or syllables making up the words or phrases at the outset, so that the learner is unsure precisely of how you verbalise certain words. The more they resort to written prompts, the more likely it is that their pronunciation will be affected by first-language interference. For most of our learners that language will be English and they will be tempted to reproduce sound patterns that belong to grapheme and to phoneme correspondences in English rather than to the target language.

We can help to reduce this barrier to learning by providing activities which draw attention to sound patterns and improve their awareness of symbol to sound correspondences in the target language. There will be some sounds which are similar to the mother tongue and some sounds which are very different, like the nasal vowels in French or *zw* and *sch* in a German word like *zwischen*.

We might ask learners to identify a sound and demonstrate that they recognise it by some form of total physical response (TPR), which could be anything from standing up and sitting down to raising a hand or touching your nose! If we are concerned that older learners may not react positively to a TPR activity, we could ask them to make a tally of how often they hear a particular sound; for instance, the phoneme *on* in a rhyme like this one:

> **Les cornichons.**
> **Ah bon!**
> **Du poisson?**
> **Non!**
> **Du jambon?**
> **Non!**
> **Du melon?**
> **Non!**
> **Des champignons?**
> **Non!**
> **Alors, quoi donc?**
> **Des cornichons!**
> **Ah bon!**

Sound raps – getting your head round phonemes!

We could set a 'beat-the-clock' challenge at the start of a lesson to find as many words including a particular sound as possible and then create a sound rap. Here is an example from a Year 10 class revising family relationships, using the sound *'ère'*:

J'aime mon père et ma mère

Ils m'ont appris à tout faire

J'aime grand-père et grand-mère et je n'oublie pas mon frère

grand-père grand-mère père mère frère (bis)

(With thanks to Claude Sgro, Abbeylands Comprehensive School, Wokingham, Surrey)

Similar approaches can be taken to onset and rime activities. Divide the class into pairs or small groups and feed in different rimes, e.g. *'une'*, *'age'*. With the help of reference materials learners can try to find as many words as they can in two minutes by adding different onsets, i.e. initial consonants or clusters of consonants that make up words, e.g. *'une' – dune, brune, prune, lune; 'age' – plage, cage, nage, sage, rage, orage.*

Again, a creative challenge could be set for either individuals or groups to come up with the longest or funniest sentence, including the most words from a particular sound bank. This could be part of a homework activity, focusing on sound and symbol correspondences and dictionary skills. For more excellent strategies for building on the National Literacy Strategy, see Cheater and Farren 2001.

Gymnastique de la mâchoire

Some of the things that learners may want to say in the normal business of classroom life, unprompted by the teacher, such as …

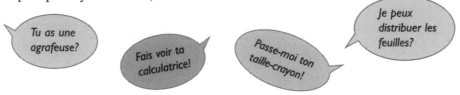

Tu as une agrafeuse?

Fais voir ta calculatrice!

Passe-moi ton taille-crayon!

Je peux distribuer les feuilles?

… may well prove a bit of a mouthful, if they have not been sufficiently well rehearsed at an earlier stage. They would benefit from some physical training to get their vocal apparatus fit for action, *'un peu de gymnastique de la mâchoire!'*.

We can help learners overcome such problems by making encounters with potentially difficult sounds 'more friendly'.

Sometimes certain words are more easily rehearsed from the rear, for example, *distribuer – er … buer … tribuer … distribuer!*

Compound words in German can be broken down into their separate parts, for example, *Tages/licht/projektor*. Imitation of each component part can start slowly from the rear and then build up in speed, like an old locomotive, until it links to the preceding component part. This process continues until all the component parts are reassembled and are readily pronounced with ease.

> *Projektor, Projektor,*
> *Licht, Licht,*
> *Lichtprojektor, Lichtprojektor*
> *Tages, Tages,*
> *Tageslicht, Tageslicht*
> *Tageslichtprojektor, Tageslichtprojektor,*
> *Tageslichtprojektor*

Any innovation is welcome if it achieves the purpose of making language accessible.

The Mexican Wave

Learners of any age rarely complain at the occasional foray into the world of football mania! We can use this intrinsic interest to our advantage and adopt the Mexican Wave as a means to rehearse aural discrimination and pronunciation. Each vertical row or column of the class responds to a separate syllable in a word by raising and lowering their arms, just as in the Mexican wave at the football stadium. Words can be chanted slowly or more rapidly, softly or more loudly and the wave can roll along the rows and back again until the sound barrier is broken and the whole word can be chanted in confidence.

The same technique can be used for whole words in sentences to enhance aural discrimination and improve pronunciation and intonation.

IMPROVING MEMORY AND ACCURACY

Improving memory is important in developing confidence and accuracy in both spoken and written communication. Simple devices borrowed from the English department can assist learners at all stages to improve memory and accuracy. In developing writing skills, learners need to be able to copy with accuracy. This seems straightforward and as we have seen, recording represents a lower-order skill in the hierarchy of thinking skills. However, the physical act of visual tracking involved in copying can prove problematic for some learners. This has serious implications for progression, if learners then attempt to memorise language from an imperfect model. If we can foster good learning habits from the outset, we can support learners to develop both accuracy and memorisation. Strategies like **Look, Cover, Write, Check** can be developed further.

The new-look vocabulary test

Recent work in Sweden involves learners in developing greater pupil autonomy in vocabulary acquisition. Examples of this technique in action are shown on the ILIAD CD-ROM (International Languages In-service at a Distance) produced in co-operation with the Open University, the BBC, CILT and a range of international partners.

The strategies used involve both individual and pairwork. In order to check out whether learners know a word, they are invited to perform four language tasks:

Teacher	Pupil
How do you know a word?	**1** *When I can say the word.*
	2 *When I can translate the word.*
	3 *When I can spell the word.*
	4 *When I can use it in a sentence.*

First this is modelled in the target language by the teacher with the whole class. It then becomes part of the learners' strategies for learning. Another interesting development is that the learners have some freedom of choice in the language that they memorise. There are core topics which everyone learns and then free-choice topics, where learners choose their own vocabulary about something which interests them. Vocabulary is tested in pairs with each partner testing the other on their chosen topic.

Vocabulaire sonore

To accompany the *dossier sonore,* familiar to us from GCSE, we might consider encouraging learners to develop their own *vocabulaire sonore.* This can form part of their homework strategies, turning vocabulary learning into a more dynamic activity – *une règle, passe-moi une règle, j'ai oublié ma règle.* Word- and sentence-level objectives can be met in this way, depending on how we or our learners choose to structure the learning. We could focus on a particular class of word, as an alternative to learning vocabulary by topic. For example, one week may have a focus on adverbs of time, the following week could be adverbs of manner. Learners memorise and record each word individually and within a sentence or short paragraph that they create for themselves.

Dictation with a difference

An activity which engages mind and body in the pursuit of memorisation and accuracy is running dictation.

Dividing the class into two circles, A and B, an inner and an outer, a short text can be photocopied several times and placed on a table or on the floor of the classroom. Learners in the outer circle have to write down the text as dictated by their partners in the inner circle who move swiftly from the text back to their partner, memorising what they have read. There is no restriction on the number of times they can return to the text or on the number of questions in the target language put to them by their partners, but the objective is to produce a fair copy of the text as fast and as accurately as they can. Points are deducted from one hundred for any mistakes made and the pair with the highest number of points wins. All manner of different texts can be used. Postcards and letters from GCSE papers, sports reports, star profiles, instructions, recipes, signs, adverts, whatever is appropriate to the topic of study. The same texts can later be exploited as stimulus material for other activities.

Simpsons on the run

Stéphanie Canicio, a graduate teacher with CILT, developed a version of the running dictation using characters from *The Simpsons*. She created four texts at different levels of complexity to suit the needs of her mixed-ability class. She divided the class into four groups, explained what the learners had to do, put the learners under starter's orders and then, they were off – Simpsons on the run! When the learners finished the dictation, they corrected it for surface features, like accents, punctuation and the accuracy of their spelling. They were then instructed to read the texts for meaning and discover if there was anything in the descriptions which was inaccurate. Of course, as these texts were created for this specific purpose, learners soon came across statements concealed in the texts which were highly unlikely, relating to Bart's TV viewing preferences and Homer's eating habits! Learners had to underline the false statements and redraft the descriptions based on what they considered to be more accurate descriptions. (With thanks to Penrice Community Language College, St Austell, Cornwall.)

Using total physical response

As learners become more mature, the way they learn needs to reflect both the level of their maturity and the complexity of the language and concepts that they are required to understand. There is a natural tendency to reduce the amount of physical engagement in the learning the older learners become, because it is felt that such approaches are more appropriate for the younger age range. Another way of looking at this could be that the contexts for active learning can become a little more sophisticated along with the learners. Using physical response to teach learners the language and process of creating a database is an example of just such a context.

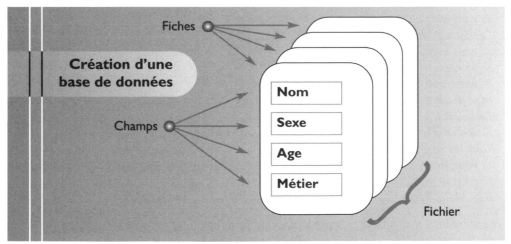

Using a diagram from information technology, which is already familiar to the learners, helps them acquire the new vocabulary. Physical engagement in response to the new vocabulary activates memory. There is also another distinct advantage. Physical movement simulating a living database offers a very simple means to understand the process of stacking and sorting information inside the memory of the computer and all that we are doing is asking learners to respond to a range of straightforward questions! Here is an example of how it is done!

Partenaires par ordinateur

The class is shown the diagram of the database to present the context and relevant language. The learners are told that an unspecified person from the Lonely Hearts column in the newspaper is seeking the perfect partner. They are invited to become a living database. In response to a range of questions they move around the room, simulating the stacking and sorting process of computer memory. The range of questions becomes increasingly more specific until just one learner fits the bill. At that point the details from the Lonely Hearts advertisement are revealed. For example:

'M' cherche le partenaire parfait. Voilà, il y a une petite annonce dans le journal. Est-ce que son partenaire parfait est ici parmi vous? On va voir!

On fait semblant. D'accord? La salle de classe s'est transformée en ordinateur. On cherche le partenaire parfait dans une base de données que nous allons créer. Vous, la classe, vous êtes les fiches dans un énorme fichier vivant. Allez-y! C'est parti!

Levez-vous!
Si vous êtes âgés de quatorze à quinze ans, restez debout!
Si vous habitez en Grande Bretagne, restez debout!
Si vous aimez la natation, allez à droite!
Si vous aimez l'informatique, allez à gauche!
Si vous aimez l'informatique et la natation, allez au milieu.
Les autres, asseyez-vous!
Si vous avez un chat, allez à gauche!
Si vous avez un chien, allez à droite!
Les autres, asseyez-vous!
Si vous avez un chat, venez au milieu!
Si vous avez les yeux bleus, allez à gauche!
Si vous avez les cheveux bruns, allez à droite!
Si vous avez les cheveux bruns et les yeux bleus, venez au milieu!
Les autres, asseyez-vous!
Si vous parlez doucement, restez debout!
Tous les garçons, asseyez-vous!
Si vous êtes bavardes, asseyez-vous!
Qui est la plus petite?
Bon, voilà, X, tu es la partenaire parfaite pour 'M', parce que 'M' c'est pour Michel! Bravo!

The stimulus for this kind of activity can vary from a real advert in a French newspaper or something reproduced in the coursebook, to something invented by the teacher or the learners.

Garçon timide de 15 ans cherche correspondante de 14 ans. Passe-temps: informatique et natation. Doit aimer les animaux – chats en particulier! Petite brune aux yeux bleus préférée – voix douce, pas trop bavarde!

A follow-up activity can be to create a database, using the language and concepts from the demonstration as a stepping stone, as an inter-class or inter-school activity or link to a partner school in France and contribute to setting up a real class exchange. Designing a database helps to develop thinking skills, as well as giving a relevant context for promoting linguistic progression. Learners must plan the structure of the database, decide on fields of enquiry, define questions necessary to elicit information, check that information is accurate, compare and contrast information to match up people to suitable partners and draw conclusions.

REPAIR STRATEGIES

When it comes to promoting the independent production of spoken language, learners need to develop repair strategies in the case of breakdown in communication and also explore ways of using what they know to convey what they don't know, sustaining communication and making new discoveries! They need to develop **strategic competence.** The mechanisms of **paraphrase** are part of this, but if learners are to develop the ability to use paraphrase readily, they must be put in situations where they have to face the unpredictable and stretch their linguistic resources.

Jeu de paraphrase

This is an enjoyable and practical activity in the form of a panel game. It requires learners to prepare clues describing a range of familiar objects, without using the appropriate name of the object itself. Instead of the name, a paraphrase is given. For example, a collection of objects, such as a corkscrew, a can opener, a paper clip, a drawing pin are gathered together. The class is divided into panels, each with a team leader. Working together, they devise the clues for each object. The structures, which teachers provide for them to use, may be at different levels of complexity:

Un trombone (a paper clip):	Eine Heftzwecke (a drawing pin):
1. c'est pour retenir des feuilles	1. damit befestigt man Papier an der Wand
2. ça sert à retenir des feuilles	2. das braucht man, um Papier an der Wand zu befestigen
3. c'est un truc qui retient des feuilles	3. ein Dings, mit dem man Papier an der Wand befestigt

The groups then stage the panel game, playing out the quiz, using the paraphrase clues and winning points by discovering the word for the object described. Dictionaries should be at the ready to verify meanings and extend vocabulary if needed.

At the most basic level, *Jeu de paraphrase* can be played by simply using the introductory structure and a non-verbal clue like a mime, e.g. *c'est un truc pour* + an action. At the most complex level, learners are using complex sentences, linked by connectives and in the case of German, using subordinate word order. The formulations used in the paraphrase are initially explicitly learned and rehearsed, but little by little they become embedded in the learners' memory and can be reproduced more automatically, indicating the increasing range of the learner's communicative competence.

Paraphrase can also be used to breathe new life into vocabulary tests. In addition to using flashcards or overhead transparencies to test vocabulary, why not use paraphrase at different levels of complexity? In a mixed ability class, it may be a suitable challenge for the more capable learners to create a set of clues for the class vocabulary test.

Y-a qu'à faire un jeu de bof/Na ja Spiel

A feature which most distinguishes the learner of the foreign language from the native speaker is the inability to flesh out the message or control the pace of an exchange. It is very revealing to listen to native speakers talking 'live' and to pick out how many expressions and exclamations are used which appear to be redundant to the central message. These expressions serve several purposes. They pad out the communication. They allow thinking time. They cover up for hesitation and they can repair a breakdown in communication. So, what sort of expressions can be used to fill in the gaps?

Keeping a class tally of expressions and exclamations heard in use by the teacher, the assistant, exchange partners or on tape or video extracts is a stimulating way of extending the range of authentic communication and repair strategies that we can borrow. For example, *J'sais pas moi*; *Si tu veux*; *Comment dirais-je?*; *Enfin*; *Bref*; *Allez*; *Non*; *Mais c'est pas ça, quoi!*; *BOF!*; *Vielleicht*; *Sicher; Weiß nicht!*; *Meinetwegen!*; *Na ja, kann sein!*; *Wirklich?*; *Mal sehen ...*

A good game can be made out of these 'fillers', *Jeu de bof/Na ja Spiel*. Learners or the teacher can put some of these expressions on card. Pupils draw one at random and are invited to build it into their GCSE role-play to add a touch of authenticity. Gradually, familiarity with the kinds of expressions used begins to permeate the learners' language and they start to use the expressions naturally as the need arises.

A variant on this is to introduce the occasional idiomatic phrase or structure and set the learners the challenge of using the phrase appropriately as many times as they can within a particular activity or sequence of activities. For instance, how many times can you use the construction *Y-a qu'à + l'infinitif* during the lesson, e.g *Y-a qu'à changer d'activité!*; *Y-a qu'à regarder dans le dictionnaire*; *Y-a qu'à faire un jeu maintenant*! Learners can either work individually and keep their own score, or they may like to run a competition in pairs and try to beat each other's scores.

THE EXTRAORDINARY SYNERGY OF INDEPENDENCE AND CREATIVITY

It can be seen that the kinds of teaching approaches most effective in developing learner independence have much in common with those which promote creativity. To succeed in developing independent use of language, we first have to stimulate the desire to communicate. Activities should entice learners to take the initiative. To progress, learners have to be willing to extend the boundaries of their knowledge and skill to the limit, generating the need for more language. To develop confidence in the use of communication strategies, they have to be put in situations where they edge forward from what is known to what is unknown, and within a supportive framework 'struggle' to convey meaning.

Here are some examples of activities which develop communication strategies and open the door to learner independence and creativity.

Points en commun/Was haben wir gemein?

If we think about a straightforward survey on a range of familiar topics – the usual things like family, pets, school subjects, hobbies – it is very unlikely that our learners will have anything much to discover about each other. This is especially so the older they get and the more time that they have spent together. In order to step up their interest and make them want to talk, we can add the magic ingredient, something secret about themselves, which can be zany or serious, according to what they are willing to reveal.

Learners interview as many people as they can in ten minutes, entering the information on a grid. In the given range of topics, most learners are rehearsing and consolidating known language, but when it comes to the secret square they are obliged to ask for clarification and use strategic competence and repair strategies in the target language in order to convey new meanings or establish understanding.

An example from a Year 10 French class:

> Elève 1:Tu as un secret?
> Elève 2: Oui, je suis 'une ceinture noire'!
> Elève 1: Une quoi? Répète, s'il te plaît! Je n'ai pas compris!
> Elève 2: Une ceinture noire. Euh! On porte une ceinture.
> Elève 1:Ah bon! On porte une ceinture, où?
> Elève 2: On porte une ceinture ici (showing his waist).
> Elève 1:Ah! Répète encore une fois! Qu'est-ce que tu portes?
> Elève 2: Une ceinture noire!
> Elève 1:Ah! Pigé! Tu fais du judo, n'est-ce pas?
> Elève 2: Oui, je fais du judo.
> Elève 1: Comment ça s'écrit?
> Elève 2: j-u-
> Elève 1: Pas judo, merci quand même! Le truc noir!
> Elève 2: c-e-i-n-t-u-r-e.

STAGE 1 > Noting new language

'New' language encountered in the process of the activity can be noted down as they go along. At this stage inaccuracies are inevitable and are an implicit part of the learning process. This is the creative bit of the learning, where learners are experimenting with language, trying out chunks of known language in new contexts, constructing new meanings, maybe inventing their own words. There is likely to be an inter-language phase, where sentences start off in one language and are completed in another. This is very useful as it gives teachers and learners a clear indication of where we should focus next.

If you wish, you can encourage your learners to use reference materials, like glossaries and dictionaries during the survey, but the results are often better if they leave the use of reference materials until a later stage in the activity, when they come to reflect on the quality of their language and write up their findings. The idea of this kind of activity is to get by with what you know and find out what you don't know.

The formative role of the teacher: our role as teachers during this stage must be to strike a fine balance between listening and evaluating their learning in order to plan the next stage of explicit teacher input and helpful intervention to improve the quality of their learning as it takes place. We have to be very skilful in how we support the interaction between pupils. Too much correction of inaccuracies as pupils engage in the activity can discourage learners from taking risks with language. If they feel that they are being tested during the activity, they will want to limit what they say to the basic question and response and 'get it right' to please the teacher. If they understand that part of the process is to discover where language runs out and what you need to learn next, then they will be more willing to have a go. If we develop a culture for learning where it is natural to explore new meanings and seek support from one another and from the teacher in using language in more open-ended contexts, we will encounter less resistance from our pupils when we ask them to try to use the foreign language throughout their activities and keep on target.

STAGE 2 > Preparing for plenary discussion

During this activity the teacher listens and notes down key questions and points for development, which can be fully explored in a whole-class discussion. Wherever possible, examples of higher quality sustained interaction from pupils can also be noted down and used in a plenary to model the language structures or communication strategies that he or she wants other learners to use. In this way, the teacher is raising the quality of pupils' learning by using examples from the peer group.

STAGE 3 > Deconstructing the learning

In the plenary, the teacher can focus on language use and the learning process by discussing with pupils, what was difficult to say, what new vocabulary was discovered, how they conveyed their meaning when language ran out. Did they use gesture and mime? Did they use paraphrase? Did they use English? If so, when? Were there particular grammatical structures which they couldn't form in the target language, which now needed to be included in the next part of the lesson?

In order to do this, we are asking our pupils to deconstruct what they have done and reflect on the learning experience. It may be appropriate for some or all of this discussion to take place in English, in order to refocus and prepare our learners for the next stage of the learning in the target language. However, gradually, in classes where the target language is becoming increasingly more established, learners can be encouraged and supported to carry out at least some parts of such discussions using the target language.

STAGE 4 > Active reconstruction

Quiz: *On fait la connaissance/Kennenlernen Spiel.* After the plenary, learners go back into groups and prepare clues for a class quiz of 'Guess who?'. Each team in turn sets the other team the challenge of identifying someone by revealing their secret but not their name. In order to gain maximum points, it is insufficient to simply hear the secret and then just name the person. Spokespersons for each team should justify their choice.

Cardinal rule: *Qui est-ce? Pourquoi? Parce que ... /Wer? Warum? Weil ...* For example:

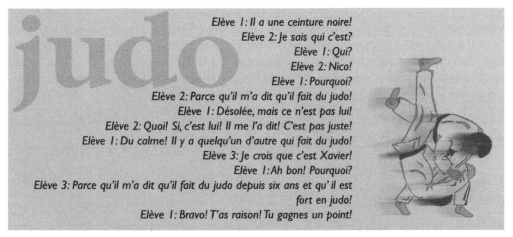

> Elève 1: Il a une ceinture noire!
> Elève 2: Je sais qui c'est?
> Elève 1: Qui?
> Elève 2: Nico!
> Elève 1: Pourquoi?
> Elève 2: Parce qu'il m'a dit qu'il fait du judo!
> Elève 1: Désolée, mais ce n'est pas lui!
> Elève 2: Quoi! Si, c'est lui! Il me l'a dit! C'est pas juste!
> Elève 1: Du calme! Il y a quelqu'un d'autre qui fait du judo!
> Elève 3: Je crois que c'est Xavier!
> Elève 1: Ah bon! Pourquoi?
> Elève 3: Parce qu'il m'a dit qu'il fait du judo depuis six ans et qu'il est fort en judo!
> Elève 1: Bravo! T'as raison! Tu gagnes un point!

We can see in this example that because the activity requires the learners not merely to state their answer but to justify it, there is a deeper engagement with the information, ideas and meaning. The language needed for justification is more complex and promotes linguistic progression as well as providing more cognitive challenge and interest.

STAGE 5 > Focus on accuracy

Following the quiz, learners work individually and write up a profile of one or more of their friends. They should have time to reflect on what they are writing and should be encouraged to add further detail, perhaps by supplying them with a writing frame to support the development of paragraphs and the use of connectives.

They may like to display their profiles as a class collage with a mixture of text and photographs. It is at this stage that they will want to refine what they are producing and will need to use dictionaries, grammatical tables, glossaries, as well as refer to their teacher or their peers using the target language in order to improve the quality of their work.

If we plan for opportunities for learners to reflect on their learning, refine their communication and consolidate learning gains, we will have helped them to move on to the next developmental stage in their language learning.

***

Developing the premise that higher-level thinking is a key factor in sustaining learner motivation, the following two activities are based on the principle of hypothesis and justification. They are intended to be carried out in small groups, as this allows learners to progress through social interaction with their peers and through sensitive intervention from their teachers or adult helpers.

Both activities are designed to provide creative contexts for the topic 'lost property'.

Objets sous pli cacheté

The individual contents of a handbag are put into numbered brown envelopes and sealed. The class is divided into groups. Envelopes are passed from group to group. Learners can feel, shake, weigh and smell the envelopes but, of course, they must not open them. They proceed by reasoning and make decisions on the nature of the object(s) within the envelope. When they make a suggestion, they must give reasons for their choice using the target language. Dictionaries are available to help them.

The multi-sensory activity is valuable for the language it stimulates and for the **social and discursive skills** which it develops:

- **expressing an opinion;**
- **disagreeing;**
- **making alternative suggestions.**

Before the learners begin the activity, the teacher models how to go about the process and engage in the discussion. This can involve just the teacher verbalising what they are doing and thinking, using expressions like, *A mon avis, je crois, je ne suis pas sûr(e), ça sent bon/mauvais, c'est grand/petit, léger/lourd, long/court, en plastique, en bois.*

If the support of a Foreign Language Assistant or sixth-form student of language is available, so that a discussion and exchange of views can be demonstrated, so much the better – *Non, ce n'est pas ça, je crois, je ne suis pas d'accord. Je crois que c'est une clef, mais je ne suis pas sûr(e) si c'est une clef de voiture ou une clef normale, disons, pour une porte d'entrée.*

The activity can be made as structured or as unstructured as necessary to suit the capabilities of the learners. It can be supported by a model dialogue in the form of a self-help sheet or overhead transparency of useful expressions or left completely open-ended. If a self-help sheet is to be used, it should never be too long or it ceases to be of value! A good compromise is to give a start on the self-help sheet, perhaps divided into three categories, some expressions of agreement, some expressions of disagreement, some adjectives to describe particular objects. There should then be space available for the learners to fill in anything else that they learn in the process of conducting the activity.

Sac perdu

This second activity lends itself to a variety of different levels of task and is intended to promote discursive language in speech and writing. Learners will engage in a series of multi-skill tasks involving reading and writing, speaking and listening, working progressively from word- to sentence- to text-level communication.

The contents of handbags or briefcases are used again. Depending on the learners, you can use real objects and provide a lost handbag or briefcase with contents for each group or put chosen contents into plastic wallets and set up the activity like a detective story with the learners sorting through the evidence. You need to provide all sorts of different objects and printed material, such as keys, wallets, spectacles, cheque-books, tickets, appointment cards, shopping lists, receipts, letters, birthday cards, telephone messages, anything that can be acquired from colleagues or the Foreign Language Assistants and is authentic and 'real'. The idea is to contrive the contents to allow learners the opportunity to construct scenarios using the notions of past, present, future and conditional. Each stage of the activity promotes thinking skills.

STAGE 1 > Recording

The first task is straightforward. The contents of the bag/wallet can be unpacked and shared around the group. From known language, learners note down items that they can already identify in the foreign language. Then, by asking each other, the assistant or their teacher, or by using reference materials, they can discover the language for the rest of the contents. They record in writing an inventory of the contents of their bag using the present tense and a list of nouns.

STAGE 2 > Reporting and generalising

The group then discusses the contents and begins to make some generalisations about the contents and the kind of person this bag may have belonged to. A spokesperson from the group then gives a report to the other groups in the class on the contents, using a combination of present tense and perfect tenses.

Il y a cinq reçus de taxis et plusieurs reçus de restaurants. C'est quelqu'un qui n'a pas de voiture. C'est quelqu'un qui mange tous les jours au restaurant. On a trouvé aussi une ordonnance pour des comprimés contre la migraine.

Depending on the amount of written material included, the activity can be organised at various levels of complexity, using various time frames. We can continue the crime theme and draw up a profile of the missing people. Who are they? What were they doing when they lost the bag? What did they buy at the supermarket? Where did they visit recently? Where will they be going soon? A range of factual information can be sought and reported back. If we are careful in our choice of contents, the learners can reconstruct the last movements of their missing person, based on the evidence provided.

STAGE 3 > Speculation and hypothesis

As an alternative we can invite our learners to become social anthropologists and speculate about the lifestyle of this person. Taking a look at the shopping list, what does this tell you about their likes and dislikes, social life, family life? Looking at the cheque-book stubs, what do they spend their money on? What kind of person are they? From reading a letter or short note, what further information can be discovered about the social history of this person, their culture and character? For example:

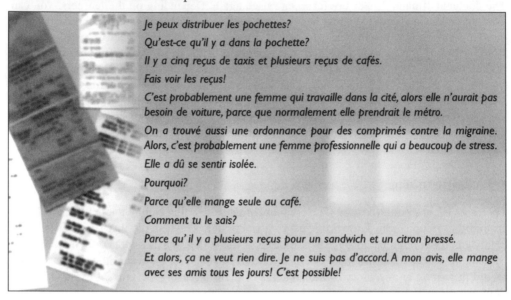

> Je peux distribuer les pochettes?
>
> Qu'est-ce qu'il y a dans la pochette?
>
> Il y a cinq reçus de taxis et plusieurs reçus de cafés.
>
> Fais voir les reçus!
>
> C'est probablement une femme qui travaille dans la cité, alors elle n'aurait pas besoin de voiture, parce que normalement elle prendrait le métro.
>
> On a trouvé aussi une ordonnance pour des comprimés contre la migraine. Alors, c'est probablement une femme professionnelle qui a beaucoup de stress.
>
> Elle a dû se sentir isolée.
>
> Pourquoi?
>
> Parce qu'elle mange seule au café.
>
> Comment tu le sais?
>
> Parce qu' il y a plusieurs reçus pour un sandwich et un citron pressé.
>
> Et alors, ça ne veut rien dire. Je ne suis pas d'accord. A mon avis, elle mange avec ses amis tous les jours! C'est possible!

This level of thinking is more demanding for the learners and develops higher-order skills. We are asking them firstly to record and report their evidence, then to generalise from it and finally to rethink their generalisations and speculate about the kind of person this could be. They are literally reworking their initial thoughts, engaging with the information more fully and deepening their understanding through hypothesis. The linguistic demands made by such activities are also of a higher and more complex nature. There are no right or wrong answers. The idea is to put forward hypotheses and test them out using the target language.

Stage 4 > Synthesis/Summing up

Although the task is carried out in small groups, learners should be taking their own notes and refining their thinking and language use as they go along. The final task is to write up their stories or hypotheses individually into a sustained and discursive piece of writing, summing up their version of events.

TAKING THE INITIATIVE

Encouraging learners to take the initiative is something to foster early on in the learning. Techniques which build on learners' ideas and enable them to transfer what they know to fresh contexts go a long way to promoting a more dynamic learning environment. Learners are more willing to take risks and volunteer contributions where they feel that their ideas are valued and are a central part of the learning process.

Techniques such as **slow-reveal**, where learners volunteer ideas in relation to the identity of a visual that is slowly revealed to them, and **prediction**, where something is hidden and learners suggest as many ideas as they can until the correct idea is given, are an essential starting point in developing independence and creativity. As the body of known language expands, we can exploit techniques such as brainstorming – *'un remue-méninges'* – more fully.

Here is a sequence of teaching and learning activities, taking place over a series of lessons.

Résidents du bâtiment B/Etagenhaus B story

The sequence begins with a demonstration involving the whole class of how to create a character from a picture. Using one of the pictures on an overhead transparency, the **slow-reveal technique** is used, covering the whole picture with a piece of card and gradually drawing back the card to reveal more and more detail progressively in response to ideas elicited from the learners.

A whole range of questions can be used, from the very simple to the more complex, to prompt suggestions and ideas from the class.

Qu'est-ce qu'il y a sous la carte? Un animal, un fruit, un légume, une personne? C'est quoi, à votre avis?
Was haben wir hier? Was für ein Bild ist das? Ein Tier, Obst, Gemüse, eine Person, oder? Keine Idee! Haben wir Vorschläge?

The card is slowly drawn down to reveal the top of the head.

Une personne? D'accord!
Genau, eine Person!

Further detail is slowly uncovered.

Un homme ou une femme? Un garçon ou une fille? Bon, oui, c'est ça, c'est une femme.
Mann oder Frau? Junge oder Mädchen? Gut, richtig. Wir haben hier eine Frau.

In the early stages of the activity the necessary scaffolding of language and concepts to answer the questions can be supplied. All the learners are required to do is to observe and select the appropriate response. During the course of the activity, as learners increase in confidence, a greater degree of choice is offered and greater scope for individual opinion is provided.

Contente ou mécontente?
Froh oder traurig?
Elle est comment, cette femme? Belle ou moche? Pourquoi?
Wie sieht sie aus? Schön oder häßlich? Warum?

Justification for the answers must always be sought. The visual is nearly entirely revealed.

Elle a quel âge? Vous avez une idée?
Wie alt ist sie? Eurer Meinung nach?

The visual is gradually completely revealed, as the class suggests possible ages.

Vingt ans, trente ans. Cinquante ans, vous dites!
Zwanzig. Dreißig. Fünfzig Jahre alt, sagt ihr?

Stage 1 > *Remue-méninges*

The whole picture is now projected. The brainstorming process has been well established by the slow-reveal technique and can be pursued further. More complex and sophisticated questions can be introduced, which make greater linguistic and cognitive demands on the learners.

Eh bien, vous avez dit cinquante ans. Pourquoi?
Warum habt ihr fünfzig Jahre alt gesagt?

The teacher gives adequate time for reflection and the formulation of appropriate reasons.

Ah! Par sa façon de s'habiller. Oui. Parce qu'elle est grosse. Elle a l'air fatiguée. Oui, elle a le front ridé. Elle porte des bottillons montants (slipper boots)*! C'est possible, oui. Dans la rue! Vous croyez?*

In the true spirit of brainstorming, all ideas are considered, certain of which are then built on to prompt further contributions and create the need for more language.

D'accord. C'est intéressant! Si je vous propose, qu'elle a trente ans. Qu'est-ce que vous diriez?
Interessant, na! Wie wäre es mit dreißig Jahre alt?

A range of opinion can be gathered from the class. Other questions can be posed in relation to the possible jobs that the characters may undertake, what kind of family they might have, their nationality, their character.

Once the class is accustomed to this style of learning, opportunities can be taken to explore stereotypes and challenge some of the more entrenched ideas expressed and a full class discussion can begin to take place with the teacher modelling the new language and feeding in new structures, enabling the learners to develop their agenda and say what they want to say.

STAGE 2 > Learning through social interaction

In the next stages of learning, there will be opportunities to work in whole-class, individual, pair and small group activities. Using the model of home groups and reconfigured groups explained in Chapter 2, p52, pupils will eventually be put into groups of six to invent their own character from a picture stimulus. Each group will have a different character to invent, so that Group A could be creating a character for a little boy with a sad face, Group B could be inventing a life style for a severe looking man with a sneer and a bald head, Group C might be trying to come up with a convincing reason why the elderly lady is wearing an overcoat and slipper boots! Each member of the group is given a copy of the same character to look at, so that the first stage of the activity can be conducted individually.

STAGE 3 > Individual work

The learners are invited to engage in the same sort of process that has previously taken place at whole-class level. They firstly have to look at their own picture and note down their ideas in draft form about the person they are creating. They are recording and describing what they see. They can then enter the realm of creativity and imagination. Who are these persons? How do they feel? Why? Do they work? If so, what do they work at? And what about their family and friends, pets and so on?

STAGE 4 > Pair work

Once individuals have noted down their initial thoughts, these are then shared with a partner. At this stage similarities and contrasts can be identified and ideas can be refined. In mixed-ability situations a great deal of support and extension can take place by sharing ideas between partners of different ability.

STAGE 5 > Pair to group work

The separate pairs then join together as a full group and present their ideas. Ideas can be judged as good or bad and retained or rejected until the group agrees their best version of a character. If there are equally strong and feasible versions, that is all to the good, they can each be respected and used for the next stage of the activity.

STAGE 6 > Plenary discussion

Time must always be allowed for learners to reflect on their learning. They require opportunities to refine what they want to say. They should have recourse to reference materials like their vocabulary books, glossaries, bilingual dictionaries, or in the case of 'slipper boots', the mail-order catalogue! As ideas are developed and refined from each group, they can be noted down on the whiteboard for all to share, as part of a plenary discussion led by the teacher.

STAGE 7 > Individual reflection

After the plenary, each individual learner must have adequate opportunity to draft and redraft a written description of the agreed character, or an individual version, if preferred. It is at this point that the principal focus of the activity is accuracy and the quality of communication. This is an opportunity to consolidate learning gains.

STAGE 8 > Reconfiguration of groups

The home groups are reconfigured (cf model pp52–53)so that each new group comprises one member from each of the original groups. We now have a situation where each individual learner has taken charge of the personality that they have created and has joined with a fresh group of learners, each in possession of a different character card. The class is then told that all of these characters live in the same block of flats, *Résidents du bâtiment B/Etagenhaus B*. They are set the task of deciding what relationships exist between the characters and to invent the introductory episode of a soap opera about them.

The process of brainstorming ideas, where each learner makes a contribution and every contribution is noted down for consideration at a later stage, is the best way of proceeding. Ideas are refined either by the learners or by the teacher. Storylines are agreed. Reference sources are in active use until a version is completed. Once again, time must be built in for a written version to be drafted and redrafted with a focus on accuracy, following a plenary discussion, where initial ideas from each group are shared and discussed.

STAGE 9 > Peer-group evaluation

The learners with their completed versions return to the home groups. Each individual learner can present their version to the home group. The group decides which version is the most exciting and why. The results of each group's deliberations are shared with the whole class and the version which has the most votes is presented to the whole class. It can later be turned into a play script and put on video, if resources allow. A selection of the soap operas can be mounted and displayed for other learners in other classes to read and enjoy.

Maximising the use of the survey

Surveys are used frequently as a means to practise simple questions and answers. In younger classes surveys usually involve everybody asking the same set of questions of everybody else. Often very little is done with the findings because the activity is more about practice than real communication. For older learners the survey can serve a much wider purpose, becoming a way-stage to producing a structured presentation on a particular topic. There is no real need for everybody to be surveying the same thing.

Using the idea of home groups, learners can prepare questions on different topics. The same process of individual, to pair, to small group work can be used to devise the questions. This allows partially developed ideas to be refined and improved by more capable learners or the teacher. Finally, within the small group as a whole, all the questions are pooled and classified into a working survey.

Surveys can be carried out in a number of ways. Learners from each home group can interview other groups within the class, or they can interview another class within the school in order to make comparisons. They can send their surveys by e-mail to the partner school abroad, or interview the exchange students.

Whether the survey is face-to-face or virtual through e-mail, with the peer group or with native speakers, what happens to the findings is crucial. A great deal of investment of time and energy has gone into the preparation of the interview grids and corresponding questions, and it is therefore more valid as an activity if an equal investment of time and energy is expended in the follow-up activities.

Each individual learner has a unique responsibility to the home group. They are team players as well as individual learners. In the process of conducting the survey they are charged with noting down the information, keeping an accurate record of what has been said and by whom. Once back to the home group, the findings can be shared and analysed. There is then opportunity for learners to make generalisations and begin to prepare their group feedback to the whole class.

Once again, the teacher will have a key role to play in how feedback is orchestrated. The teacher will know from his or her observation of how the groups have been operating who has produced work of the highest quality and who is the most likely to be able to report back cogently. The teacher will also have identified language needs that will require further support, perhaps remodelling by examples taken from the small group interaction. It is probably best if it is the teacher who structures the feedback by choosing individual learners to contribute their ideas. Questions for clarification or repetition from other learners should as far as possible be in the target language.

After the plenary discussion, learners in each home group prepare a structured talk from notes on the topic that they have researched. As a final activity, written reports in the form of a newspaper on all of the different topics can be compiled and circulated to every learner.

FEATURES OF ACTIVITIES WHICH HELP LEARNERS KEEP ON TARGET

The kinds of processes used in these activities develop creativity and independence. Emphasis is placed on mutual respect for the ideas and contributions of others, as well as on linguistic progression. Within the different stages of the activities there is a shifting emphasis from encouraging the expression of ideas, which stretch linguistic resources and result in a degree of 'formative error', to the focus on the refinement of form and attention to accuracy, supported by the teacher and more capable peers.

There are messages for the changing role of the teacher in this approach. If the teacher intervenes too swiftly or comes across as too critical, this may result in curbing learners' initiative and readiness to say what they want to say. The teacher needs to create positive attitudes to error and a learning environment where learners feel comfortable to experiment with language. As they refine the content of their contributions for specific purposes, they will seek to express themselves as coherently and accurately as possible. They will invite intervention, because they have invested in the learning process and thought about what they want to say.

It is the learners who are setting the pace and the direction of the activities, and the approach to grammar and accuracy is more 'learner driven.' Professor Hawkins raises the importance of pupil feedback and curiosity driven exploration of grammar in his paper 'Percept before precept' (King and Boaks 1994).

These activities serve as examples and may or may not appeal to all teachers or indeed to all learners. What is of interest is that they have some or all of these features in common.

They:

- combine two or more of the four language skills;

- allow learners to move from what is known to what is unknown, dealing gradually with more complex language and tasks;

- stimulate interest in using reference sources;

- offer opportunities to use repair strategies and communication strategies, developing learners' potential to solve linguistic problems and deal with the unpredictable;

- develop discursive skills, for example, expressing agreement and disagreement, making suggestions, taking turns;

- offer a range of different writing opportunities, from noting down information from spoken input, noting down discoveries from reference sources, collecting ideas from discussion, to drafting and redrafting creative writing, to making a written presentation or delivering a structured talk from notes;

- foster constructive attitudes towards error, which can be seen as a way-stage towards greater accuracy, appropriate to audience and purpose in both spoken and written communication;

- widen the learners' range of structure and vocabulary according to the learners' agenda as well as the teacher's;

- engage learners in higher-order thinking skills which promote their cognitive development;

- offer learners the chance to explore their own culture or that of the countries where the target language is spoken.

We can see that progress is being made in all four attainment targets through the promotion of active involvement and the development of interaction in the target language. Our learners are beginning to step beyond the basic response.

3 You speak, they speak: focus on planning

Enabling learners to say what they want to say, as well as to say what we want them to say, requires very careful and systematic planning. Saying the first thing that comes into our heads or, indeed, verbalising everything indiscriminately will not in itself enable learners to become independent users of the language, despite the alluring title of this *Pathfinder.*

In terms of classroom language and the management of learning, we need to be selective and focused about what we say and how we say it. The simpler we can be to start with the better! We have to make decisions about what is essential for learners to use and understand and what is less important. We can analyse language and make decisions about which structures have greater currency for our learners and can choose formulations which can be readily adapted by them for their own use.

There is much that we can do to support learners' linguistic progression by both implicit and explicit teaching. If we are using the target language as the natural means of communication in our classroom, we can plan for progression in our own use of target language in such a way that pupils will be able to systematically borrow structures from the teacher stimulus and manipulate them to their own purposes. The language of teacher instruction can be recycled into the learners' repertoire.

Here is an example where one learner is remodelling the written work of others in the group. He modifies and extends a familiar imperative structure and frequently used expression that he has acquired through listening to his teacher's use of the target language, e.g.

| *Mettez vos sacs par terre!*
Ce n'est pas la fin du cours! | **becomes** | *Mettez un 'e' à la fin du participe passé parce que*
le sujet est féminin. |

We can see further examples of this in the pupil to pupil interactions described in some of the activities in the previous chapter.

The learner in the role of the teacher in the Quiz on p65 is recycling teacher language: *Du calme! Bravo! T'as raison! Tu gagnes un point!*

The learners interacting with one another in the small group activity described on p68 are reformulating teacher language:

| *Fais voir ton cahier!* | **becomes** | *Fais voir les reçus!* |

| Tu peux distribuer les feuilles? | becomes | Je peux distribuer les pochettes? |

| Qu'est-ce qu'il y a sous la carte? | becomes | Qu'est-ce qu'il y a dans la pochette? |

This has been made possible because of sustained use of the target language by teachers and learners from the outset of their learning.

CONSISTENT APPROACHES FROM ONE CLASS TO ANOTHER

Within the classroom, where the explicit aim is for pupils themselves to use the target language for real purposes, strategies which encourage pupils to share in the control and management of learning bring a number of instant advantages. The language of classroom routines, instructions, demonstrations, evaluation, praise and discipline need to be in regular use from class to class. If we have been consistent, particularly in the early years, in the choice of language we use, learners will gain confidence in using and responding to the target language in a variety of situations.

The more consistent we are, the more the divisions of responsibility for the day-to-day business of the classroom between teacher and learner can become progressively more blurred. Learners can be invited to assume the role of the teacher, giving instructions, demonstrations and explanations to the whole class and to their partners. How we set up opportunities for them to use the target language for genuine purposes with their partner is the key to progression. They can organise their own resources, choose their own partners or groups, discuss and evaluate their work, using a defined range of language from a very early stage. The language necessary to do this can be explicitly taught and will gradually become more automatic over time.

TASK-SPECIFIC LANGUAGE

Language needs will vary from one activity to the next. As learners progress, the complexity of higher-order language activities will require a greater range of language to explain the process. If learners are to be involved in using the target language, both as the medium as well as the object of study, careful analysis of the language required to set up and conduct activities should be taking place regularly from lesson to lesson. As we plan our lessons and scheme of work, it may be valuable to think of such language as a discrete area of content, entitled perhaps 'task-specific language'. Learners should be reminded that language use is the means to an end as well as the end itself. Task-specific language will be of equal importance as any other area of content. It should be as simple and unambiguous as possible at the start and will become increasingly more complex as learners progress. Some of this language will develop 'naturally' as the learners process the language they hear being used by their teachers. They will also begin to transfer language from the set-piece defined content that they are learning from their coursebooks and GCSE topics. But much of this language can also be pre-taught.

TEACHING INTERACTION LANGUAGE

An impressive example of this comes from a special school teaching German to all pupils from 11–16. Here the teacher uses a lot of competitive games to motivate her learners. In order to encourage them to use the target language throughout the lesson, she pre-teaches the language that they will need to interact with one another in particular learning contexts. For example, if she is going to use a dice game, she plans a sequence of lessons building up to this and pre-teaches in a variety of whole-class and pair-work activities the language of turn-taking, expressions of anger, pleasure, frustration as well as how to manage the game itself before they play. In this way, it is expected that during the game learners interact for the most part in German – and they do!

RESPONDING TO LEARNERS' NEEDS

As we plan our lesson content, we will need to consider the kinds of special language that learners might require in order to express themselves and function as a responsible partner or member of a group. The development of social skills required to design and agree questions in a group to draw up a survey, for example, needs to go hand in hand with the analysis of the language required to carry out the activity. If our aim is that our learners should increasingly employ the target language to carry out transactions, instructions and requests, the necessary language will need to be progressively built into our teaching programmes. It is in this immediate context of social interaction in the here and now that we can begin to develop socio-linguistic competence for real.

THE QUERY OVER GRAMMAR

Can we develop grammatical awareness without recourse to English? There are times when it is appropriate to put words under the microscope and study elements of language in relation to form. We might, for example, take a familiar text and invite learners to play the 'grammar detective' and extract all the adjectives or verbs denoting actions that happened in the past and ask them to investigate the words, recognise patterns and deduce rules. The fact that they have 'discovered' the pattern for themselves, formulated a provisional rule and then tested it out by finding other examples within the text is a powerful agent in securing grammatical understanding and progression.

It is part of the cognitive process of learning a second language that comparisons and parallels will be drawn from knowledge and experience of the first language. It may be that some of the grammatical analysis is quite properly undertaken for a short time in English in the interests of developing effective language awareness, perhaps building on the legacy of the National Literacy Strategy.

There may be times when two-language conversations work to good effect, where the learner is using English but the teacher responds in the target language. We can afford to be pragmatic. The kind of analytical activity described above can occupy a valuable place in language learning, providing that there are swift follow-up opportunities to match linguistic discoveries to real purposes and set language forms into living functional communication in the target language.

As the culture of using the target language becomes more established and 'natural', learners will gradually feel ready to discuss their discoveries using the target language and these discussions will become part of the content of the lesson.

The following transcript is taken from a plenary discussion during a Year 10 German class. The teacher is trying to establish whether the class has fully understood the new structure *um … zu* (with grateful thanks to Natalie Schlatter, a graduate teacher at Haydon Language College, Pinner). These learners are second foreign language learners and have two twilight sessions per week. Their teacher is an Austrian national and insists on the rigorous use of the target language throughout the lesson.

Also, was haben wir heute gelernt?

Wir haben einen Dialog gemacht und wir haben Gesundheit diskutiert.

Ja, kannst du erklären?

Ja, wir wissen jetzt was man machen muss, um gesund zu bleiben!

Gut! Kannst du ein Beispiel geben?

Ja, um schlank zu bleiben, esse ich wenig Fett.

Andere Vorschläge?

Ja, um gesund zu bleiben, mache ich viel Sport.

Um ungesund aber glücklich zu sein, sehe ich viel fern und esse ich Schokolade!

Habt ihr neue Wörter gelernt?

Ja, wir haben um … zu gelernt.

Und wir verstehen was ein Infinitiv ist.

Also, was ist ein Infinitiv?

Das Verb bevor es 'changes'? Wie sagt man 'changes'?

Das Verb ohne Person.

Ja, richtig! Der Infinitiv ist das Verb bevor es sich ändert.

An impressive example, which shows it can be done!

4 Prompts for self-evaluation and future action

If we want to create a classroom culture where communication in the target language is perceived as a shared objective, successful planning will involve ourselves, our colleagues and above all our learners. We could make a start by asking ourselves the following questions in relation to the range and scope of our current teaching practices:

■ TEACHER USE OF THE TARGET LANGUAGE

- Is there a departmental policy on using the target language?

- Do we have consistent approaches towards how we give objectives and set up language-learning activities using the target language?

- Do we review our use of the target language in order to introduce structures which have the greatest currency for re-use by our learners?

- Do we plan for progression in our use of the target language, starting with simple structures and moving on to the more complex?

- Do we pre-teach task-specific and interaction language that we expect our learners to use in carrying out activities in the classroom?

- Do we involve our learners in developing their own strategies to promote greater use of the target language?

■ QUESTIONING

- How do we use questioning?

- Do we use closed questions where we expect a set answer?

- Do we use staged questioning, offering alternatives?

- Do we use open-ended questions where a range of answers is acceptable and there are no right or wrong answers?

- Do we only use questions to rehearse and test vocabulary or unanalysed chunks of new language or do we also use questions where we have an interest in the answers given and develop the learning around these?

- Are questions always set at a low level of cognitive challenge or do they require learners to think about their answers and use more complex language to convey their meaning?

- Do learners have the opportunity to ask questions of the teacher and of each other?

WHAT IS OUR APPROACH TO GRAMMAR?

- Do learners have opportunities to explore and experiment with language and discover patterns and grammar rules for themselves?

- Is grammar always studied out of context?

- Are discussions about language structures, patterns and rules always conducted in English or are discussions conducted in the target language, or in a mix of both?

- How much meta-language is used, e.g. verb, noun, adjective? Is any of this in the target language?

- Who initiates discussions about grammar, the teacher or the learners?

- Do we discuss progression in language learning with colleagues in the English department in order to build on current developments in Literacy?

HOW DO WE STRUCTURE THE LEARNING?

- Is the lesson teacher driven or are there opportunities for learners to build on their own ideas?

- Is there a balance between whole-class, individual, pair and group activities?

- Do we provide sequences of activities, which support learners to move from simple to complex use of language?

- Do we involve our learners at all stages of the learning, drawing on their creativity and imagination, involving them in 'linguistic problem-solving' not merely in reproducing stock answers?

- Do we offer them opportunities to learn from one another?

- Do we provide sufficient challenge in the learning tasks to stimulate **'cognitive conflict'** and move our learners on to the next stage?

- Do we give them formal opportunities to reflect on their learning, reformulate ideas and consolidate learning gains?

- What is our approach to error? How do we model and improve pupil use of the target language? When and how do we intervene during pair and group work?

How do we plan for linguistic progression?

Do we provide a balance of activities which:

- 'Train the ear' developing learners' abilities to discriminate particular sounds?

- 'Train the eye' focusing on sound and symbol correspondences as well as sound and meaning?

- Encourage awareness of pattern, making learners aware of function and form?

- Allow learners to rehearse 'chunks of language' in familiar contexts?

- Challenge learners to experiment with language in fresh contexts by deconstructing and reconstructing memorised 'chunks'?

- Enable learners to reflect on the language they are using and develop their grammatical competence, making the language-learning process the content of our lesson?

- Offer opportunities to communicate for different purposes and to different audiences, including their peers in this country and in the country where the target language is spoken?

- Develop strategic competence by encouraging the use of communication strategies such as combinations of verbal and non-verbal communication, circumlocution, paraphrase, enabling learners to deal with the unpredictable?

- Develop the effective use of reference sources, using dictionaries skilfully?

- Promote the use of complex sentences linked by connectives?

- Provide opportunities to hold conversations, sequence their ideas, give structured talks, stage an argument, persuade, discuss in pairs and in groups?

Conclusion:
back to the future

Developing a culture where it becomes increasingly more automatic and natural for learners as well as teachers to operate through the target language is a complex matter. There are many factors which we need to take into account. Among these will be the different learning styles of our pupils, their prior experience of the target language and the whole issue of rich and stimulating content. We must make sure that we are giving them something worthwhile to communicate about. The more relevant the input is to the learner, the more likely it is that input will become intake.

We will also need to consider the nature of the challenge itself and what we understand of the principles of learning and how these relate to second-language learning. We should be mindful that second-language learning is a different process from first-language acquisition. To quote Hawkins (King and Boaks 1994):

> '*Getting the L2 in class, in x short weekly lessons, is quite unlike the infant's subconscious acquisition of the mother tongue. There are now several modes of cognition in play. Deliberate learning complicates the process at every stage.*'

What we are trying to do in our classroom is to plan for progression through a dynamic process involving both deliberate and conscious language learning and spontaneous language use, a process described by Stevick (1982) as a continuum. This mirrors Johnstone's premise (1989) that: '*there are two complementary sides to communication: one being intuitive and spontaneous and the other being analytical and reflective.*'

Professor Hawkins again:

> '*Across this continuum the learner's strategies range, subtly interacting with each other. Deliberately learned routines can become subconscious, available without thinking one moment, but requiring deliberate recall the next. Explicit and implicit knowledge of grammar rules weave in and out of each other, while comparisons with the mother tongue are never far away.*'

For learners to make progress in using the target language requires more than just making language memorable and asking our learners to reproduce 'chunks of language' in response to a set-piece stimulus, although this is in itself part of the process. Moving on will entail a fine balance between allowing learners to experiment with language without feeling inhibited by fear of error and their need to have opportunities to reflect on their learning, discuss language forms and ask questions.

We will need to provide appropriate 'scaffolding'. This can come in a number of forms: the way we accustom their ear to new sounds; the way we present and rehearse new language to facilitate pronunciation, memorisation and re-use; the way we use questioning, moving from staged questioning with alternatives to more open-ended questioning; the way we set up pair and group work to include genuine interaction and discussion; the kinds of reference and self-help materials that we make available; the type of tasks that we require them to engage in; our approach to grammar. We will need to make explicit our increasing expectations of the learners to use the target language independently both in their interactions with us and with their peers.

Meeting the challenge of using the target language for the purposes of all classroom communication can begin with a deceptively simple task; that of sitting around the table with colleagues and thinking more systematically about the most commonly used structures and phrases in our teaching. If we get this right, little by little, layer upon layer, we can build on this foundation and model pupil use of the target language from the stimulus that we have provided. In so doing, we can develop their knowledge and understanding about language itself and help them towards greater independence.

By gradually extending the range and quality of learning opportunities that we offer our learners, language learning can also contribute to developing their strategic competence and their creativity, helping them to solve problems, structure their ideas and develop thinking skills.

By reviewing the nature of the content of our teaching programme, we can enable our learners to make new discoveries through the target language which are of personal relevance to them and make a contribution to other areas of the curriculum and to their social development.

The central message is that teachers cannot control learning. Learning is something that learners do for themselves, not something that is done to them. What we can do is to support the learning process by planning an appropriate structure for learning and providing a rich and diverse range of experiences which might just enable learners to learn more effectively.

What we all aspire to do is to produce learners who, at the end of their period of language study, can say what they want to say and are still hungry to learn more. Let us hope that some of the ideas and strategies described here can go some way to helping us towards this aim.

* Bibliography

Bachman, L. F. (1990) *Fundamental considerations in language testing.* Oxford University Press.

Bachman, L. F. and Palmer A. S. (1996) *Language testing in practice.* Oxford University Press.

Bloom, B. S. (ed.) (1956) *Taxonomy of educational objectives: the classification of educational goals: Handbook I, Cognitive domain.* Longmans Green.

Canale, M. (1983) 'From communicative competence to communicative language pedagogy'. In Richards, J. C. and Schmidt, R. W. (eds), *Language and communication,* 2–27. Longman.

Canale, M. and Swain, M. (1980) 'Theoretical bases of communicative approaches to second language teaching and testing'. *Applied Linguistics* 1, 1–47.

Cheater, C. and Farren, A. (2001) Young Pathfinder 9: *The literacy link.* CILT.

Halliwell, S. (1993) *Grammar matters.* CILT.

Hawkins, E. (1987) *Modern Languages in the curriculum.* Cambridge University Press.

Johnstone, R. (1989) *Communicative interaction: a guide for language teachers.* CILT.

King, L. and Boaks P. (1994) *Grammar! A conference report.* CILT.

Little, D. (1999) *Strategies in language learning.* CILT.

Vygotsky, L. (1978) *Mind in society.* Harvard University Press.

Vygotsky, L. (1986) *Thought and language.* MIT Press (original work published in 1934).

Wood, D., Bruner, J. S. and Ross, G. (1976) 'The role of tutoring in problem-solving'. *Journal of Child Psychology and Psychiatry.*

classic pathfinder

Classic Pathfinders

deal with those MFL issues that will never go away. Based on the wisdom contained in the best-selling titles in the series, the material has been re-written and updated by the original authors in the light of the challenges of today's classroom. Each title contains re-editions of two related titles in the *Pathfinder* range which are truly 'classic'.

Classic Pathfinders are for:

- experienced teachers refreshing or renewing their practice – particularly as they go into positions of leadership and need to articulate the principles of good practice;
- newly qualified or beginner teachers who want to build up the essentials of good language-teaching methodology.

Classic Pathfinder 2

Challenging classes: focus on pupil behaviour

Jenifer Alison and Susan Halliwell

This book focuses on disaffected or potentially disruptive pupils. It sets out practical ways of engaging them and helping them to succeed in their language learning. The publication provides a timely reappraisal of how we can address the inclusion agenda in the MFL classroom through motivating activities and strong classroom management.

New Pathfinders

provide an expert MFL perspective on national initiatives. They are designed to support the language-teaching profession by ensuring that MFL has its own voice and ideas on the issues in education today.

New Pathfinders provide user-friendly support, advice and reference material for today's CPD agenda.

New Pathfinder 1

Raising the standard: addressing the needs of gifted and talented pupils

Anneli McLachlan

The author presents a strategic approach to tapping the potential of high-ability pupils. She shows how re-analysing teaching and learning styles to cater for the most able can help raise the standard of all learners.

'Pathfinders *get better and better. This* Pathfinder *is excellent'*

Jane Jones, Head of MFL Teacher Education, King's College London

New Pathfinder 2

The language of success: improving grades at GCSE

Dave Carter

This book presents strategies to help all students achieve their best possible grade at GCSE.